The Dudley Genealogies and Family Records

Dean Dudley

BIBLIOLIFE

The Ruins of Dudley Castle in Staffordshire, England. See page 79.

THE

DUDLEY GENEALOGIES

AND

FAMILY RECORDS.

Arms borne by the Hon. Thomas Dudley, first Dep. Gov. and second Gov. of Mass. Bay.

BY DEAN DUDLEY.

"Children's children are the *crown* of old men;
And the glory of children are their fathers."

———

BOSTON:
PUBLISHED BY THE AUTHOR.
1848.

PREFACE.

The Work,

Here presented, is intended as an introduction to a large *biographical* account of the Dudley family, which I have long been collecting, and design to publish on my return from Europe, whither, I am about to proceed for the purpose of extending my researches further, than is practicable in this country.

It seemed expedient to publish this collection thus early, in order, that an opportunity might be offered for the correction of unavoidable errors and the addition of such records, as might be found wanting in the genealogies. And, therefore, it is earnestly desired, that those, possessing additional records or corrections of errors, will forward them to me, as soon as possible ; and all appropriate biographical sketches will, also, be received with much gratitude. I am not unmindful of past favors, but tender my warmest thanks to those, who have, already, lent their assistance in this arduous undertaking.

It will be seen that some of the genealogical accounts, given in this volume, are more extensive and much nearer complete than others. This difference is owing entirely to the facilities, that have been afforded for obtaining the necessary facts ; and not to any preference of my own, and, hereafter, I hope to be able to make the whole complete and perfect.

I am particularly desirous of ascertaining the precise relationship between the different branches of the Dudley family in this country ; and I trust the necessary evidence will yet appear to prove them all of one great family, descended from a common ancester by the name of Sutton of Dudley castle.

In the next volume, the sources from which these collections have been obtained, and the authors consulted, will be minutely specified.

Perhaps it may not be out of place to add here, that, in transcribing old records, where double dates occur, I have omitted the date of the former year, and only copied that of the year according to New Style. For the early settlers, of this country, till about 1700, reckoned time according to Old Style, and began the year on Lady Day, the 25th of March; but during the first half of the 18th century, for events occurring between January 1st, and March 25th, two dates were given, as on page 77, of this volume,—the former for the Julian year, begining March 25th,—the latter, for the Gregorian, beginning January 1st.

But there is another difference between Old and New Style; for the Julian year, which contained 365 days and 6 hours, exceeding the Solar year, in length, a little more than 11 minutes, had therefore fallen behind it about 10 days, in 1582, when pope Gregory XIII. reformed the calender, and dropped the ten days from it. But, as England and her colonies did not adopt the New Style till the 18th century, the Julian year was eleven days behind the Gregorian, and constantly receding. Hence, to change Old Style to New, 10 days must be added to dates in the 16th or 17th century, (a less number to earlier dates)—11 to those in the 18th, and the Russians, who still use the Old Style, must add 12 days to their dates in the present century, to make them accord with New Style.—*See Am. Quar. Regr. Vol. XIV. p.* 254.

D. D.

Cambridge, Sept. 1, 1848.

CONTENTS OF THE VOLUME.

PART FIRST.

PART SECOND.

DUDLEY GENEALOGIES.

PART FIRST.

DUDLEY ARMS.

DUDLEY (Willingham house, Co. of Cambridge, bart.) Sa. on a fesse ar. between two lions passant in chief and a sinister hand bendways, couped at the wrist in base or buck courant gu.

Crest—A buck's head erased or attired sa. the neck transpierced with an arrow barbed and flighted ppr. and gorged with a collar gu. pendent therefrom an escutcheon of the second, charged with a hand as in the arms.

DUDLEY (of Berkshire and Buckinghamshire) az. chev. engr. voided or.

DUDLEY (of Clapton, Co. of Northampton) az. a chev. or. between three lions' heads.

DUDLEY (of Staffordshire) or. two lions pass. az.

DUDLEY, (the same within a bordure) az.

Crest—out of a viscount's coronet or. pearled ar., a lion's head az. collared of the first.

DUDLEY, the same *Arms*, the bordure engr.

Crest—out of a ducal coronet, or. a lion's head az. collared, and ringed of the first.

DUDLEY, az. a chev. between three lions' heads erased or.
DUDLEY, or. a lion ramp. vert. (another, the tail forked.)
DUDLEY, or. two bends az.
DUDLEY, ar. a cross former az.
DUDLEY, ar. on a chief az. three crescents or.
DUDLEY, az. a chev. engr. or.

Explanation of Some of the Terms of Heraldry.

Or., a yellow color or gold. Of precious stones, the To-
paz is its equivalent,—of the planets, Sol, (the sun.)
Ar., a white "color" or silver. Of precious stones, the
Pearl is its equivalent,—of the planets, Luna, (the
moon.)
Sa., a black color. The Diamond equals it in precious
stones,—the planet Saturn.
Gu., a red color, the Ruby, Mars.
Az., blue, the Sapphire, Jupiter.
Vert., green, the Emerald, Venus.
Purp., purple, the Amethyst, Mercury.
Tenné, tawny, the Jacinth, Dragon's head.
Sanguine, murrey, the Sardonix, Dragon's tail.

Dudley Cognomen.

The surname of "Dudley" was taken from the castle of
Dudley, in Staffordshire, and assumed, according to an-
cient custom in England, by the younger children of the
Barons of that place. The Castle of Dudley was built by
Dudo, an English Saxon, about A. D. 700.

First Generation in England.

HUGH DE SUTTON was a native of Nottinghamshire, England. He married Elizabeth, dau. and heir of William Patrick, lord of the moiety of the Barony of Malpas, Chester Co.

Second Generation.

THE SON OF HUGH DE SUTTON,

RICHARD DE SUTTON, likewise of Nottinghamshire, Eng., m. Isabel, only dau. and heir of Rotheric, the son of Griffin.

Third Generation.

THE SON OF RICHARD DE SUTTON,
SON OF HUGH DE SUTTON,

SIR JOHN DE SUTTON, *Kt., first Baron of Dudley*, m. Margaretta De Somerie, sister and co-heir of John De Somerie, lord Dudley, and, probably, lived and died at the town of Dudley, Eng.

Fourth Generation.

THE SON OF SIR JOHN DE SUTTON, KT., 1st B.,
SON OF RICHARD DE SUTTON,

JOHN DE SUTTON, *second Baron of Dudley*, m. Isabel, dau. of John De Charlton, lord Powis, and died A. D. 1376, at Dudley.

Fifth Generation.

THE SON OF JOHN DE SUTTON, 2d B.,
Son of John De Sutton, Kt., 1st B.,

John De Sutton, *third Baron of Dudley*, m. Elizabeth, dau. of Edward, lord Stafford, and died A. D. 1406, at Dudley.

Sixth Generation.

THE SON OF JOHN DE SUTTON, 3d B.,
Son of John De Sutton, 2d B.,

John De Sutton, *fourth Baron of Dudley*, Lord Lieutenant of Ireland, was born A. D. 1401, and died in the early part of the reign of *Henry the Sixth*.

Seventh Generation.

SON OF JOHN DE SUTTON, 4*th B. of Dudley*,
Son of John De Sutton, 3*d B.,*

John Sutton, *fifth Baron of Dudley, Kt. of the most noble Order of the Garter*, and Treasurer of the King's household, m. Elizabeth Berkley, widow of Sir Edward Charlton, and dau. of Sir John Berkley of Beverston, Co. of Gloucester, Kt.

Eighth Generation.

CHILDREN OF JOHN SUTTON, Kt., &c., 5*th B. of Dudley*, Son of John De Sutton, 4*th B.*,

Sir Edmund Sutton, lord Dudley, m. 1st, Joice Tiploft, sister and co-heir of John T., Earl of Worcester; 2d, Maud, dau. of Thomas, lord Clifford;

JOHN SUTTON, Sir John Dudley, Kt., m. Elizabeth Bram-
shot, dau. of John B. of Bram., Co. of Sussex, Kt.;
WILLIAM SUTTON, *lord Dudley, Bishop of Durham*, died
A. D. 1483, at London;
MARGARET SUTTON m. Sir George Longueville of Little
•Billing, Northamptonshire.

Ninth Generation—First Family.

CHILDREN OF SIR EDMUND SUTTON,

Lord Dudley, SON OF JOHN SUTTON, KT., &c., 5th B.,

EDWARD DUDLEY, *sixth Baron of Dudley*, m. Cecily Wil-
loughby, dau. of Sir William Willoughby, and died
A. D. 1530;
JANE DUDLEY m. William Middleton, Esq.;
THOMAS DUDLEY m. the daughter and co-heir of Lance-
lot Threlkeld, Esq. of Torworth;
Rev. RICHARD DUDLEY;
MARGARET DUDLEY m. Edward, lord Powis;
ALICE DUDLEY m. Sir John Ratcliffe;
DOROTHY DUDLEY m. Sir John Musgrave, Kt.

Second Family.

CHILDREN OF JOHN SUTTON, SIR JOHN DUDLEY,

Kt., SON OF JOHN SUTTON, KT., &c., 5th B.,

ELIZABETH m. Thomas Ashburnham;
EDMUND DUDLEY, a lawyer and statesman, was born A. D.
1462, m. 1st, Ann Windsor, dau. of Sir Andrews
Windsor, and widow of Sir Roger Corbet of Mor-
ton; 2d, Elizabeth Grey, dau. of Sir Edward Grey,

Viscount L'Isle, A. D. 1494. This lady, for a 2d husband, m. Arthur Plantagenet. Dudley was beheaded August 18, 1510, at London.

Tenth Generation—First Family.

CHILDREN OF EDWARD DUDLEY, 6th B. of Dudley, Son of Sir Edmund Sutton, lord Dudley,

John Dudley, *seventh Baron of Dudley*, m. Cicely Grey, dau. of Thomas Grey, Marquis of Dorset;

Jane Dudley m. lord Dacre;

Alsanore Dudley m. Charles Somerset, Earl of Worcester;

Catharine Dudley m. George Gresley;

Elizabeth Dudley m. Sir John Huddlestone, Kt.;

Joice Dudley.

Second Family.

CHILDREN OF THOMAS DUDLEY, Son of Sir Edmund Sutton, lord Dudley,

Richard Dudley;*

Two other sons, one of whom may have been Capt. Roger Dudley;§

Three daughters, whose names are unknown to me.

---

* It is well known that this gentleman left a numerous posterity.

§ This is mere supposition. However, Capt. Roger, the father of our Gov. Thomas, was cotemporary with the sons of this Thomas Dudley, and it was then, as well as at the present time, very customary for parents to bestow, on their children, the Christian names of *the grandparents.* Thus, our Gov. Thomas *might* have received the name of his grandfather, the Thomas Dudley mentioned above.

Third Family.

CHILDREN OF EDMUND DUDLEY, Lawyer, only Son of John Sutton, *Sir John Dudley, Kt.,*

John Dudley, *Duke of Northumberland,* was born A. D. 1502, at London ; m. Jane Guilford, dau. of Sir Edward Guilford, and was beheaded August 22, 1553, at London ;

Sir Andrew Dudley died 1559, at *London, Tothill Street ;*

Jerome Dudley died at London, quite aged ;

Elizabeth Dudley m. William, sixth lord Stourton.

Eleventh Generation—First Family.

CHILDREN OF JOHN DUDLEY, *7th B.,* Son of Edward Dudley, *6th B. of Dudley,*

Edward Dudley, *eighth Baron,* m. 1st, Catharine Brydges, lady Chandos ; 2d, lady Jane Stanley ; 3d, Mary Howard ;

George Dudley ;

Henry Dudley ;

Dorothy Dudley ;

Elizabeth Dudley.

Second Family.

CHILDREN OF JOHN DUDLEY, *Duke of Northumberland,* son of Edmund Dudley, Lawyer,

Henry Dudley was slain at the siege of Boulogne, aged 19 years ;

Thomas Dudley died at London, aged 2 years;

John Dudley was born 1530, at London, m. lady Ann
   Seymour, dau. of Sir Edward Seymour, Duke of
   Somerset, June 3, 1550, died without issue Oct. 21,
   1554, at London;

Ambrose Dudley, Earl of Warwick, was born 1531, at
   London, m. 1st, Ann Thorwood; 2d, Elizabeth Tab-
   lois; 3d, lady Ann Russel;

Robert Dudley, Earl of Leicester, m. 1st, Amy Robsart,
   June 4, 1550; 2d, lady Douglass Sheffield, dau. of
   Wm. lord Howard; 3d, lady Lettice Devereux,
   dau. of Sir Francis Knolles, and widow of Robert
   Devereux, Earl of Essex;

Guilford m. lady Jane Grey, dau. of Henry Grey,
   Duke of Suffolk, and was beheaded Feb. 12, 1554,
   at London. His wife, the lady Jane, was also beheaded at London on the same day;

Henry Dudley, 2d, m. Margaret Audley, dau. of
   Thomas, lord Audley. He was slain at the siege of
   St. Quintins, 1557;

Charles Dudley died, aged 4 years, at London;

Mary Dudley m. Sir Henry Sidney;*

Margaret Dudley died, aged 10 years, at London;

Catharine Dudley m. Henry Hastings, Earl of Hunt-
   ingdon;

Temperance Dudley died, aged 1 year, at London;

Catharine Dudley, 2d, died, aged 7 years, at London.

---

* The accomplished Sir Philip Sidney was their son.

Twelfth Generation—First Family.

CHILDREN OF EDWARD DUDLEY, 8th *Baron of Dudley,*

ANN DUDLEY m. Thomas Wilmer, Esq.;

EDWARD DUDLEY, *ninth Baron of Dudley*, m. Theodosia Harrington, and died A. D. 1643;

JOHN DUDLEY m. ———.

Second Family.

THE ONLY SON OF AMBROSE DUDLEY, EARL OF WARWICK,

JOHN DUDLEY died in childhood.

CHILDREN OF ROBERT DUDLEY, EARL OF LEICESTER,

SIR ROBERT DUDLEY, a son of lady Sheffield, was born in 1573, at Sheen, in Surry, m. 1st, Miss Cavendish; 2d, lady Alice Leigh; 3d, Mrs. Elizabeth Southwell, whom he espoused, while his first wife was still living. He died at Florence, in Italy, and lies buried at Boldrone, Italy;

ROBERT DUDLEY, a son of lady Essex, died in childhood, July 15, 1584.

Thirteenth Generation—First Family.

CHILDREN OF EDWARD DUDLEY, 9th *Baron of Dudley,*

SIR FERDINANDO DUDLEY, KT., m. Honora, dau. of Edward, lord Beauchamp, July 16, 1610;

2

LADY MARY DUDLEY m. James, Earl of Hume, Scotland ;

LADY ANN DUDLEY m. Meinhardt, Count Schomberg ;

LADY MARGARET DUDLEY m. Sir Miles Hobart, K. B.

Second Family.

CHILDREN OF SIR ROBERT DUDLEY, SON OF ROBERT DUDLEY, EARL OF LEICESTER,

ALICE DUDLEY never was married ;

DOUGLAS DUDLEY   do. ;

CATHARINE DUDLEY m. Sir Richard Leveson, K. B., and died at Trentham, Co. of Stafford, Feb. 1673 ;

FRANCES DUDLEY m. Sir Gilbert Kniveton ;

ALEZIA DUDLEY never was married. She died May 23, 1631, at London ;

ANN DUDLEY m. Sir Robert Holbourne ;

CHARLES DUDLEY, a son of Sir Robert, by his second wife, Elizabeth, m. Mary Magdalen Gouffier, of France ;

One daughter, by the second wife, m. the Prince of Piombino ;

One daughter by do. m. the Marquis of Chivola ;

One   "   by do. m. the Duke of Castillion del Lago ;

One   "   by do. m. the Earl of Carpegna.

Fourteenth Generation—First Family.

DAUGHTER OF SIR FERDINANDO DUDLEY, KT.,

FRANCES DUDLEY m. Humble Ward, who was created Baron of Dudley in 1644, in right of his wife. This lady died 1697.

Second Family.

CHILDREN OF CHARLES DUDLEY, SON OF SIR ROBERT DUDLEY, *Son of Robert Dudley, Earl of Leicester,*

ROBERT DUDLEY;

A son, who was an ecclesiastic in France;

A daughter, who m. 2d, the Marquis Palliotti, of Bologna, Italy.

———

Posterity of Thomas De Dudley.

THOMAS DE DUDLEY, lord, descended from the Suttons, Barons of Dudley, died at Clapton, Co. of Northumberland. His grandson m. Agnes Hotot, heiress of the ancient family of Hotot, 1395.

From this marriage descended,—Sir William Dudley, Esq., who m. 1st, a dau. of M. de Pleure; 2d, Jane, dau. of Sir Roger Smith, Kt.; 3d, Mary, dau. and heiress of Sir Paul Pindar, Kt., and died A. D. 1670, at Edmonthorp, Leicestershire.

THE CHILDREN OF SIR WILLIAM, ESQ., (which were by his third wife,) were :—

SIR MATTHEW, Bart., m. lady Mary O'Bryen, dau. of Henry, Earl of Thomond, and died April 13, 1721;

WILLIAM, *rector* of Clapton, died, unmarried, May, 1726;

MARY m. Sir John Robinson, Bart.

THE CHILDREN OF SIR MATTHEW, Bart.,
were:—

Sir William, Bart., m. Elizabeth Kennedy, dau. and sole heir of Sir Richard K., Bart., of Ireland, and died June 15, 1764, aged 63 years;

Sarah Henrietta.

THE CHILDRFN OF SIR WILLIAM, Bart., were:—

O'Bryen, William, and Elizabeth, who all died, unmarried, before their father.

THE POSTERITY OF GOV. THOMAS DUDLEY,

THROUGH HIS ELDEST SON,

REV. SAMUEL, OF EXETER, N. H.

~~~~~~~~~~~~~~~

CAPT. ROGER DUDLEY* was slain in "the wars" in early life, about A. D. 1586, leaving only two children, a son and a daughter, viz.:

THOMAS, (1)§ b.   A. D. 1576, at Northampton, Eng., d. July 31, 1653, at Roxbury, Massachusetts ;

A daughter, b.   probably at Northampton, Eng., d. at ——, England, as we believe.

Marriages.

GOV. THOMAS m. 1st, Dorothy ———, who died Dec. 27, 1643, aged 61 years, at Roxbury; 2d, Mrs. Catharine Hackburn, April 14, 1644, who survived him, and m. for her third husband, Rev. John Allen, of Dedham, Mass., by whom she had children.

---

* Capt. Roger could not have belonged to the *Duke of Northumberland's* branch of the Dudley family.

§ Thomas Dudley came over to this country in 1630. Though most of his children were born in England, his family is accounted the first of the name in America, because all lived and died here, as we have good reason to believe. Possibly, however, some might have died in childhood before the family came across the Atlantic.

First Generation in America.

CHILDREN OF THOMAS, (1) Son of Roger,

Children by the first wife. [*]

> SAMUEL, (2) b.   , 1606, at Northampton, Eng.,
> d. Feb. 10, 1683, at Exeter, N. H. ;
>
> ANN, b.   1612, at Northampton, Eng., d. Sept.
> 16, 1672, at Andover, Mass. ;
>
> PATIENCE, b.   , at Northampton, Eng., d.   ,
> 1690, at Ipswich, Mass. ;
>
> MERCY, b. Sept. 27, 1621, at Northampton, Eng., d.
> July 1, 1691, at Newbury, Mass. ;
>
> SARAH, b.   , at Northampton, Eng., d.   ,
> 1668, at Roxbury, Mass. ;

By the second wife.

> DEBORAH, b. Feb. 27, 1645, at Roxbury, d.   ;
>
> JOSEPH,§ b. Sept. 23, 1647, at Roxbury, d. April 2,
> 1720, at the same town ;
>
> PAUL,§ b. Sept. 8, 1650, at Roxbury, d. Dec. 1,
> 1681, at Boston, Mass.

Marriages.

REV. SAMUEL m. 1st, Mary Winthrop, dau. of Gov.
John W., in 1633, at Cambridge, Mass. ; 2d, Mary
———— ; 3d, Elizabeth ————. The first wife died
April 2, 1643, at Salisbury, Mass. The second and
third died at Exeter, N. H. They all had children ;

---

[*] All these children of Gov. Thomas, by his wife, Dorothy, had
posterity.

§ For the posterity of these two *younger* sons, see the SECOND PART.

ANN, the Poetess, m. Gov. Simon Bradstreet, in 1628,
    doubtless at Northampton, Eng.   Gov. B. survived
    her, and m. a second wife, who was a dau. of
    Emanuel Downing, and died at Salem, Mass. ;

PATIENCE m. Maj. Gen. Daniel Dennison, at Cambridge,
    Mass. ;

MERCY m. Rev. John Woodbridge, of Newbury, Mass.,
    in 1641. ;

SARAH m. 1st, Maj. Benj. Keayne, who returned to Eng-
    land, and repudiated his wife for alleged inconti-
    nence ; after which, she married Mr. Pacy ;

Gov. JOSEPH m. Rebecca Tyng, dau. of Hon. Edward T.
    This most worthy and accomplished lady died Sept.
    21, 1722, aged 71 years ;

PAUL, merchant of Boston, m. Mary Leverett, dau. of
    Gov. John L.

Second Generation in America.

CHILDREN OF SAMUEL, (2) SON OF THOMAS, *son*
of Roger,

Children by Mary, dau. of Gov. Winthrop.

‡THOMAS, bap. March 9, 1634, at Cambridge, Mass.,
    d. Nov. 7, 1655, at Boston, Mass. ;

JOHN, bap. June 28, 1635, at Cambridge, Mass.,
    d.   at —— ;

MARGARET, bap.   at Cambridge, Mass., d.   at
    Salisbury, Mass. ;

SAMUEL, bap. Aug. 2, 1639, at Cambridge, Mass., d.
    April 17, 1643, at Salisbury, Mass. ;

ANN, b. Oct. 16, 1641, at Salisbury, Mass., d.   ,
    at —— ;

I believe these to have been all the children by Mary, the 2d wife of Rev. Samuel Dudley.

†THEOPHILUS, b. Oct. 31, 1644, at Salisbury, Mass.,
d.   1713, at Exeter, N. H.;

MARY, b. April 21, 1646, at Salisbury, Mass., d. Oct.
28, 1646, at Salisbury, Mass.;

‡BILEY, b. Sept. 27, 1647, at Salisbury, Mass., d.
about 1728, at Exeter, N. H.;

MARY, 2d, b. Jan. 6, 1649, at Salisbury, d.
at ——;

THOMAS, 2d, b.   , at Exeter, N. H., d.   , 1713,
at ——;

Probably these were the children by Elizabeth, the third wife.

STEPHEN, (3) b.   , at Exeter, N. H., died   ,
1734, at Exeter, N. H.;

‡JAMES, b.   , 1663, at Exeter, N. H., d. Nov. 14,
1720, at Exeter, N. H.;

TIMOTHY, b.   , at Exeter, N. H., d.   , at ——;

ABIGAIL, b.   , "   do.   do. d.   , " ——;

DOROTHY, b.   , "   do.   do. d.   , " ——;

REBECCA, b.   , "   do.   do. d.   , " ——;

ELIZABETH, b.   , "   do.   do. d.   , " ——;

SAMUEL, 2d, (4) b.   , at Exeter, N. H., d. 1732, at
the same town.

Marriages.

ANN m. Col. Edward Hilton, of Exeter, N. H.;

CAPT. THEOPHILUS never was married;

BILEY, Esq., m. Elizabeth Gilman, Oct. 25, 1682;

MARY, 2d, m. Samuel Hardie, a Schoolmaster some time
of Beverly, Mass.;

THOMAS, 2d, m. Mary ——, and they were living at
Exeter, A. D. 1697;

STEPHEN, Esq., m. 1st, Sarah Gilman, dau. of Hon. John G.,
Dec. 24, 1684. She was born Feb. 25, 1667, and
died Jan. 24, 1713. 2d, Mary Thing; 3d, Mercy
Gilman, who survived him;

LIEUT. JAMES, merchant, m. Elizabeth Leavitt, dau. of
Samuel L. This lady survived him, and m. 2dly,
Robt. Briscoe, Oct. 8, 1724, whom she also sur-
vived; and 3dly, Rev. John Odlin;

ABIGAIL m. Mr. Watson;

DOROTHY m. Moses Leavitt, Oct. 26, 1681;

REBECCA m. Francis Lyford, Nov. 21, 1681;

ELIZABETH m. Capt. Kinsley Hall, Sept. 25, 1674. Capt.
Hall died about 1736;

SAMUEL, 2d, m. Hannah ——— ;

The rest probably died young and unmarried.

Third Generation in America.

CHILDREN OF STEPHEN, (3) SON OF SAMUEL, (2) *Son of Thomas,* (1)

SAMUEL, (5) b. Dec. 19, 1686, at Exeter, N. H., d. Feb.
16, 1718, at Exeter;

STEPHEN, (6) b. March 10, 1688, at Exeter, d.   , 1734,
at E.;

JAMES, (7) b. June 11, 1690, at Exeter, d.   , at the
same town;

†JOHN, b. Oct. 4, 1692, at Exeter, was killed by the Indians, A. D., 1710, at Poplin, N. H.;

3

NICHOLAS,(8) b. Aug. 27, 1694, at Exeter, d. July, 1766,
    at Brentwood,* N. H.;
JOANNA, b. May 3, 1697, at Exeter, d.   , at E.;
SARAH, b. Jan. 15, 1706, at Exeter, d.   , at ——;
TRUEWORTHY, (9) b.   , 1700, at Exeter, d.   , 1745,
    at E.;
JOSEPH,(10) b.   , 1702, at Exeter, d.   , 1731, at E.;
ABIGAIL, b.   , at Exeter, d.   , probably at E.;
ELIZABETH, b.   , at Exeter, d.   , doubtless at E.

Marriages.

SAMUEL m. Hannah Colcord, Nov. 24, 1709, at Exeter;
STEPHEN, cordwainer, m. Sarah Davidson, dau. of Daniel
    D., July, 1708, at Newbury, Mass.;
LIEUT. JAMES, cooper, m. Mercy Folsom, dau. of Dea.
    John F., of Exeter;
NICHOLAS, Esq., m. Elizabeth Gordon;
SARAH m. Maj. Ezekiel Gilman;**
CAPT. TRUEWORTHY m. Hannah Gilman, dau. of John G.;
JOSEPH m. Maria Gilman, Nov. 26, 1724. This lady m.
    for a 2d husband, Philip Conner, May 14, 1729.
JOANNA m. Nicholas Perryman, Esq., a lawyer, of Exeter;
ABIGAIL m. Mr. Lyford, of Exeter;
ELIZABETH m. Simon Gilman.

---

* This town was formerly a part of Exeter. I am quite sure these
children were all by the first wife.

** MAVERICK Gilman m. one " Sarah Dudley," and it is possible I
may have confounded the two names.

CHILDREN OF SAMUEL, 2d, (4) Son of Samuel, (2)
Son of Thomas, (1)

†Samuel, b.   , at Exeter, N. H., d.   , about 1758, at Exeter;

Jonathan, (11) b.   , at Exeter, d. June, 1762, at Brentwood, N. H.;

Mercy, b.   , at Exeter, d.   , at——;

†Joanna, b.   , at Exeter, d.   , at——;

†Elizabeth, b. Feb. 9, 1714, at Exeter, d. about 1762, at E.

Sarah, b. April 9, 1716, at Exeter, d.   , at——;

Mary, b.   , at Exeter, d.   , at——.

Marriages.

Jonathan, Esq., m. Dinah Bean, dau. of John Bean, Oct. 13, 1720;

Mercy m. Mr. Thing, of Exeter;

Mary m. Mr. Watson;

Sarah m. Mr. Leavitt.

Fourth Generation in America.

CHILDREN OF SAMUEL, (5) Son of Stephen, (3)
Son of Samuel, (2)

John, (12) b. June 22, 1711, at Brentwood, d. Nov. 6, 1786, at Brentwood;

Samuel, b. Feb. 9, 1714, at Brentwood, d.   , at B.

Hannah, b. April 9, 1716, at Brentwood;
Samuel, 2d, (13) b. Aug. 26, 1718, at Brentwood, d. Dec.
    15, 1787, at B.

Marriages.

Capt. John m. Elizabeth ———;
Hannah m. Josiah Thing;
Hon. Samuel, 2d, m. Deborah Gilman, Aug. 4, 1748.

CHILDREN OF STEPHEN, (6) Son of Stephen, (3)
Son of Samuel, (2)

Samuel P., (13½) b.   , 1721, at Exeter, d. Jan. 9, 1789,
    at Andover, N. H.;
Davidson, (14) b.   , at Exeter, d. about 1787, at
    Brentwood, N. H.;
Stephen, (15) b. Oct. 14, 1724, at Exeter, d. Aug. 22,
    1811, at Gilmanton, N. H.;
Paul, (16) b.   , at Exeter, d.   , at ———;
Margaret, b.   , at do.   d.   , at ———;
Sarah, b.   , at do.   d.   , at ———;
Joanna, b.   , at do.   d.   , at ———;
Abigail, b.   , at do.   d.   , at ———;

Marriages.

Samuel P. m. Jane Hubbard, who d. at Andover, N. H.,
    July 17, 1814, aged 89 years and 7 months;
Davidson, blacksmith, m. Anna Ladd;

Dea. Stephen m. Hannah Sanborn,* dau. of John S., Jan. 1745 ;

Margaret m. Francis Becket, of New Jersey.

' CHILDREN OF JAMES, (7) Son of Stephen, (3) *Son of Samuel,* (2)

James, (17) b.   , 1715, at Exeter, d. May 1761, at Brentwood, N. H. ;

Abigail, b. Oct. 31, 1716, at Exeter, d. Nov. 18, 1802, at Boston, Mass. ;

Samuel, (18) b.   , 1720, at Exeter, d. Aug. 30, 1797, at ——, Me. ;

John, (19) b. April 9, 1725, at Exeter, d. May 21, 1805, at Raymond, N. H. ;

Joseph, (20) b.   , 1728, at Exeter, d.   , 1792, at Raymond, N. H. ;

Joanna, b.   , at Exeter, d.   , at Deerfield, N. H. ;

†Sarah, b.   , at do. d.   , at —— ;

Mercy, b.   , at do. d. at ——.

Marriages.

James, cooper, m. Deborah Bean ;

Samuel, Esq., m. 1st, Miss Ladd ; 2d, Mrs. Sleeper ; 3d, Mrs. Clark ;

Hon. John m. Elizabeth Gilman, dau. of Caleb G. Esq., June 22, 1749, at Exeter. She died, 1806, aged 79 years ;

Joseph m. Susanna Lord ;

---

* This lady died March 11, 1816, at Gilmanton.

ABIGAIL m. Aaron Young, who was born Oct. 27, 1714,
    and died April 1, 1789 ;

JOANNA m. Daniel Ladd ;

MERCY m. Mr. Emerson ;

SARAH was never married.

CHILDREN OF NICHOLAS, (8) SON OF STEPHEN, (3)
Son of Samuel, (2)

†JOHN, b.   , 1723, at Brentwood, N. H., d.   , 1796,
    at ——, Conn. ;

BILEY, (21) b.   , 1725, at Brentwood, d.   , at Fish-
    erfield, N. H. ;*

TRUEWORTHY, (22) b.   , 1727, at Brentwood, d.
    1759, at Exeter, N. H. ;

JOSEPH, (23) b.   , 1728, at Brentwood, d.

SARAH, b.   , at Brentwood, d.   , at —— ;

BETSEY, b.   , at do. d.   , at —— ;

NICHOLAS, b.   , at do. d.   , at —— ;

Marriages.

BILEY m. 1st, Miss Stone ; 2d, Mrs. Lufkin ;

TRUEWORTHY, blacksmith, m. Miss Gordon ;

JOSEPH m. Hannah Leavitt. He was in the French and
   Revolutionary wars ;

SARAH m. Capt. Josiah Robinson ;

BETSEY m. Mr. Hill ;

NICHOLAS m. Abigail ——.

---

* This town is now called Newbury.

CHILDREN OF TRUEWORTHY, (9) Son of Stephen, (3) *Son of Samuel,* (2)

Gilman, (24) b. May 3, 1727, at Exeter, d. June 12, 1803, at Sanbornton, N. H.;

Trueworthy, (25) b.   , at Exeter, d. about 1778, at ——, N. Y.;

Hannah, b.   , at Exeter, d.   , at —— ;

Dorothy, b. about 1739, at Exeter, d. about 1824, at Gilmanton, N. H.

Marriages.

Gilman m. Sarah Conner,* of Exeter, who d. Oct. 7, 1812;

Trueworthy, a soldier, m. Patty Gilman;

Hannah m. Caleb Thurston;

Dorothy m. John Kimball.

CHILDREN OF JOSEPH, (10) Son of Stephen, (3) *Son of Samuel,* (2)

Sarah, b. Sept. 25, 1725, at Exeter, N. H., d. Aug. 30, 1742, at Exeter;

Eleanor, b.   , at Exeter, d. at ——.

Marriage.

Eleanor m. Thomas Kimball, Sept. 25, 1746, at Exeter.

---

* I have been told her name was " Maria;" but, on the records of Sanbornton, it is written " Sarah."

CHILDREN OF JONATHAN, (11) Son of Samuel, (4)
Son of Samuel, (2)

John, (26) b. Dec. 25, 1745, at Brentwood, N. H.; d.
     May 27, 1773, at Brentwood;

†Jonathan, b.   , at Brentwood, l. A. D., 1772, at B.;

Elizabeth, b.   , at Brentwood, d. May 27, 1809, at
     Gilmanton, N. H.;

Sarah, b.	, at Brentwood, d.	, at ——;
Dinah, b.	, at do.	d.	, at ——;
Mercy, b.	, at do.	d.	, at ——;
†Samuel, b.	, at do.	d.	, at ——;
Catharine, b.	, at do.	d.	, at ——;
Hannah, b.	, at do.	d.	, at ——;
†Joanna, b.	, at do.	d.	, at ——.

Marriages.

John m. Sarah Folsom, Nov. 1, 1768;

Elizabeth m. Joseph Greely, Jr., Dec. 2, 1741;

Sarah m. ~~Derby~~ Kelley; *D*2 ιο *δ* ιι

Dinah m. J. Johnson;

Mercy m. 1st, Mr. Hunneford; 2d, Mr. Johnson;

Catharine m. 1st, Mr. Severance; 2d, Mr. Hidden;

Anna m. Mr. Kimball;

Jonathan lived to an old age, but never was married.

Fifth Generation in America.

CHILDREN OF JOHN,* (12) Son of Samuel, (5) *Son of Stephen,* (3)

Samuel, (27) b.   , 1738, at Brentwood, N. H., d. Dec. 21, 1789, at B.;

John, (28) b.   , at Brentwood, d. Oct. 5, 1802, at B.;

Winthrop, (29) b. Dec. 17, 1749, at Brentwood, d. Feb. 11, 1820, at B.;

Hannah, b.   , at Brentwood, d.   , at Gilmanton;

Elizabeth, b.   , 1739, at B., d. Jan. 27, 1753, at B.;

Anna, b.   , at Brentwood, d.   , at B.;

†Sarah, b. Dec.   , 1742, at Brentwood, d. Dec. 26, 1814, at B.;

Mary, b.   , 1746, at Brentwood, d. Dec. 11, 1813, at Newburyport, Mass.

Marriages.

Hon. Samuel m. Rebecca Lyford, who died at Brentwood, April 10, 1782;

John m. Joanna Gilman, dau. of Jeremiah G., of Waterford;

Capt. Winthrop m. Hannah Stephens, Dec. 20, 1776;

Hannah m. Jonathan Thing;   } *Brothers;*
Anna m. John Thing, A. D., 1760, }

Mary m. 1st, Maj. Porter Kimball, of Newbury, Mass.; 2d, Daniel Dodge, of the same town.

---

* His wife was a daughter of Col. Winthrop Silsby.

4

CHILDREN OF SAMUEL, (13) SON OF SAMUEL, (5)
Son of Stephen, (3)

JOSIAH, (30) b. May 20, 1749, at Brentwood, N. H., d.
Aug. 1, 1826, at B. ;

SAMUEL, (31) b. Aug. 28, 1753, at Brentwood, d. Oct. 14,
1781, at B. ;

HANNAH, b. July 9, 1751, at Brentwood, d.   , at B.

Marriages.

JOSIAH m. Mary Chase ;

SAMUEL m. Mary Leavitt;

HANNAH m. Jonathan Sleeper.

CHILDREN OF SAMUEL P., (13½) SON OF STE-
PHEN, (6) *Son of Stephen,* (3)

JEREMY, (31¼) b. 1756, at Hawk,* N. H., d. Aug. 1823, at
New Hampton, N. H. ;

HUBBARD, (31½) b. Feb. 18, 1764, at Hawk, d. Dec. 13,
1841, at Durham, L. C. ;

JACOB,** b. 1766, at Hawk, l. 1848, at Hanover, N. H. ;

STEPHEN,§ b.   , at Hawk, l. do. at Danbury, N. H.

Marriages.

JEREMY m. Polly Roberts ;

HUBBARD m. Sarah Ingalls, Jan. 8, 1789 ;

---

* This town is now called Danville.

** Jacob has seven sons, names unknown.

§ Stephen has two daughters, do.

JACOB m. Mehitable Scribner, of Andover;
STEPHEN m. Abigail Fellows.

CHILDREN OF DAVIDSON, (14) SON OF STEPHEN, (6)
Son of Stephen, (3)

‡DAVIDSON, b.   , at Brentwood, N. H., d.   1775,
    at Cambridge, Mass.;

STEPHEN, (32) b.   , at Brentwood, d.,   , at ——,
    Co. of York, Me.;

TIMOTHY, (33) b.   , at Brentwood, d. 1776, in the
    army, at ——, N. J. or N. Y.;

‡TRUEWORTHY, b.   , at Brentwood, d. 1776, at Cam-
    bridge, Mass.;

†DAVIZION, b.   , at Brentwood, d. about 1757, at ——,
    near Canada E.;

PETER COFFIN, (34) b.   , at Brentwood, d. at ——,
    Co. of York, Me.;

PEGGY, b.   , at Brentwood, d. at ——;

ANNA, b.   , at   do.   d. at ——;

LEVI, b.   , at   do.   d. at ——.

Marriages.

STEPHEN, blacksmith, m. Phebe Webster, of Brentwood;

TIMOTHY, a soldier of the Revolution, m. Mary Leavitt,
    of Brentwood;

PETER COFFIN m. Polly Perry, of Watertown, Mass.;

PEGGY m. Nathaniel Chase, of Brentwood;

ANNA m. Walden Webster, of Brentwood;*

DAVIDSON died without issue in the Revolutionary army, at Cambridge, Mass.;

DAVIZION likewise left no issue. He was slain by the Indians in the last French war, on the frontier of Canada East;

TRUEWORTHY died in the Revolutionary army at Cambridge, leaving no family.

CHILDREN OF STEPHEN, (15) SON OF STEPHEN, (6)
Son of Stephen, (3)

NICHOLAS, b.   , at Exeter, d.   , at Barnstead, N. H.;

JOHN, (35) b. Sept. 15, 1748, at Exeter, d.   , at Gilmanton, N. H.;

SAMUEL, (36) b. March 9, 1751, at Exeter, d.   , April 10, 1776, at Gilmanton;

MEHITABLE, b.   , at Exeter, d.   , at Alton, N. H.;

DANIEL, b.   , at ——, d.   , at   do.;

STEPHEN, b.   , at ——, d.   , at ——;

SARAH, b.   , at ——, d.   , at ——;

PETER, (37) b. Sept. 19, 1767, at Gilmanton, d.   , at G.

Marriages.

JOHN m. Olive Kimball, of Exeter, Oct. 16, 1771;

SAMUEL m. Sarah Clough, May 7, 1771;

PETER m. Susan Lougee,§ Aug. 14, 1788.

---

* Probably some of the others were married, but I know not to whom.

§ This lady was born, March 8, 1764.

CHILDREN OF PAUL, (16) Son of Stephen, (6)
Son of Stephen, (3)

PAUL, b.   , at Sanbornton, N. H., d.   , at ——;
HUBBARD, b.   , at ——, d.,   , at ——;
ABIGAIL, b.   , at ——, d.   , at Sanbornton, N. H.

Marriage.

ABIGAIL m. John Dudley, son of James D.

CHILDREN OF JAMES, (17) Son of James, (7)
Son of Stephen, (3)

JAMES, (38) b.   , at ——, d.   , at ——, Canada E.;
ELIPHALET, b.   , at ——, d.   , at ——, in youth;
STEPHEN, (39) b.   , at ——, d.   , at Readfield, Me.;
†JONATHAN, b.   , 1752, at ——, d.   , 1776, in the
   army of the Revolution, at Ticonderoga, N. Y.;
JOHN,* b.   , at ——, d.   , 1776, at ——;
HANNAH, b.   , at ——.

Marriages.

JAMES m. Miss Glidden;
STEPHEN m. Miss Sleeper;
JOHN m. Abigail Dudley, dau. of Paul D.;
HANNAH m. Mr. Gilman.

---

* This gentleman had a small family, but their names are unknown to me.

CHILDREN OF SAMUEL, (18) Son of James, (7)
Son of Stephen (3)

DANIEL, (40) b. about 1744, at Raymond, N. H., d. July
20, 1811, at ——— ;

SAMUEL, (41) b.   , at ———, d.   , 1795, being drowned
in Sheepscot river, Me. ;

MICAJAH, (42) b.   , 1750, at ———, d.   , 1789, at
———, Me. ;

JEREMIAH, (43) b.   , 1753, at ———, d.   , at Bath,
N. Y. ;

MOSES, (44) b.   , 1755, at ———, d.   , at ——— ;

ELIPHALET, (45) b.   , 1759, at ———, d.   , at ———,
West Virginia ;

JAMES, (46) b.   , 1761, at ———, d.   , 1809, at Hamp-
den, Me. ;

MARY, b.   , at ———, d.   , at ——— ;

MEHITABLE, b.   , at ———, d.   , at ——— ;

LYDIA, b.   , at ———, d.   , at ——— ;

Marriages.

DANIEL m. Miss Dinsmore ;

SAMUEL m. Miss Sarah Young, dau. of Aaron Young ;

MICAJAH m. Miss ——— ;

JEREMIAH m. Miss ——— ;

ELDER MOSES m. Miss Sleeper ;

ELIPHALET m. Miss Gilman ;

JAMES m. Miss ——— ;

MARY m. Mr. Haines ;

MEHITABLE m. Mr. Stephens;

LYDIA m. Mr. Ingraham.

CHILDREN OF JOHN, (19) SON OF JAMES, (7) *Son of Stephen*, (3)

JOHN, b. Dec. 29, 1751, at Exeter, N. H., d. Aug. 16, 1752, at E.;

JOHN, 2d, (47) b. Jan. 15, 1754, at Exeter, d. Dec. 1828, at Mt. Vernon, Me.;

JAMES, (48) b. Oct. 4, 1761, at Exeter, d.   , at Raymond, N. H.;

NATHANIEL, (49) b. Nov. 25, 1763, at Exeter, d. May 7, 1844, at Freeman, Me.;

MOSES, (50) b. Jan. 29, 1766, at Exeter, d. July 2, 1843, at Raymond, N. H.;

BETSEY, b. May 14, 1750, at Exeter, d. July 18, 1751, at E.;

ELIZABETH, b. May 18, 1756, at Exeter, d. January, 1832, at ——;

SUSANNA, b. July 3, 1759, at Exeter, d. at Raymond, N. H.

Marriages.

CAPT. JOHN, 2d, m. Susanna Smith;

JAMES m. Polly Stephens;

HON. NATHANIEL m. 1st, Anna Smith, dau. of Nicholas Smith, Nov. 27, 1783; 2d, Mrs. Harriet Pulling, January 26, 1826;

HON. MOSES m. Nancy Glidden, who died April 1, 1843, at Raymond, N. H.;

Elizabeth m. Thomas Bean;

Susanna m. Col. Theophilus Lovering, who is living at Raymond, 1848.

CHILDREN OF JOSEPH, (20) Son of James, (7)
Son of Stephen, (3)

Joseph, (51) b. Feb. 15, 1750, at Exeter, N. H., d. Oct. 28, 1825, at Raymond, N. H.;

†Benjamin, b.   , 1753, at Exeter, d.   , 1795, at Mt. Vernon, Me.;

Thomas, (52) b. Nov. 18, 1766, at Exeter, d. Mar. 28, 1839, at Chester, N. H.;

Daniel b.   , 1768, at Exeter, d.   , 1813, at Chester;

Elizabeth, b.   , 1752 at Exeter, d.   , at Mt. Vernon, Me.;

Joanna, b.   , at Exeter, d.   , at Candia, N. H.;

Mary, b.   , at   do.,   d.   , at Gilmanton, N. H.

Hannah, b.   , at do.,   d.   , at Raymond, N. H.

Susannah, b.   , at do.,   d.   , at Vershire, Vt.

Marriages.

Elder Joseph m. 1st, Deborah Bean; 2d, Sarah Smith;

Thomas m. Mary Moody;

Daniel m. 1st, Sarah Glidden; 2d, Miss Brown;

Elizabeth m. Samuel S. Gilman;

Joanna m. Reuben Bean;

Mary m. Nathaniel Wells;

Hannah m. Nathan Robie;

Susannah m. Jonathan Gilman.

CHILDREN OF BILEY, (21) SON OF NICHOLAS, (8)
Son of Stephen, (3)

†JONATHAN S., b.   , at ——, d. in the Revolutionary army, in N. Y.;

TRUEWORTHY, (53) b.   , at ——, d.   , at ——;

SARAH, b.   , at ——, d.   , at —— ;

JOHN, b.   , at ——, d.   , at ——.

Marriage.

TRUEWORTHY m. 1st, Sarah ———, of Roxbury, Mass., who died Nov. 14, 1791; 2d, Anna McWilliams, Oct. 10, 1792.

CHILDREN OF TRUEWORTHY, (22) SON OF NICH-
OLAS, (8) *Son of Stephen*, (3)

NICHOLAS,* b.   , at Brentwood, N. H., d.   , at ——, Conn.;

†JOHN, b.   , at Brentwood, d.   , at Epping, N. H.

Marriage.

REV. NICHOLAS, a graduate of Harvard University, m. Miss Barton, of Connecticut.

---

* This gentleman left a numerous family in Connecticut, but their names are unknown to me.

5

CHILDREN OF JOSEPH, (23) Son of Nicholas, (8)
Son of Stephen, (3)

Joseph, b.   , at Brentwood, N. H., d.   , at ——,
    West Indies;

Samuel, b.   , at Brentwood, d.   , at ——;

Ephraim, b.   , at do.,   d.   , at ——, Ohio;

Elizabeth, b.   , at do.,   d.   , at ——;

Trueworthy, (54) b. Jan. 5, 1757, at Brentwood, d.   ,
    at ——, Co. of York, Me.;

†Hannah, b.   , at Brentwood, d.   , at ——;

Patty, b.   , at do.,   d.   , at Exeter, N. H.;

Martha, b.   , at do.,   d.   , at ——;

Sarah, b.   , at do.,   d.   , at Epping, N. H.

Marriages.

Trueworthy, a soldier of the Revolution, m. Miss S. Stephens;

Patty m. Jonathan Lovering;

Martha m. Mr. Blake;

Sarah m. Mr. Page, of Epping, N. H.

CHILDREN OF GILMAN, (24) Son of Trueworthy, (9) Son of Stephen, (3)

Trueworthy, (55) b. Sept. 23, 1753, at Exeter, N. H.,
    d. Nov. 10, 1846, at Pembroke, N. H.;

Samuel C., (56) b. Aug. 12, 1764, at Candia, N. H.,
    l. 1848, at Sanbornton, N. H.;

Sarah, b.   , at Candia, d.   , at ——;

HANNAH, b.　, at Candia, d.　, at C.;

MARIA, b.　, at Candia, l. 1848, at Thornton, N. H.;

ANNA, b. Aug. 22,　, at Candia, d.　, at ——;

†MARY, b. June 23, 1771, at Candia, d. June 26, 1830, at Sanbornton, N. H.

Marriages.

TRUEWORTHY m. 1st, Hannah Knox; 2d, Sarah H. Rowell;

SAMUEL C. m. Mercy Thorn, Oct.* 1790;

SARAH m. Reuben Smith;

HANNAH m. Henry Clark, of Candia, N. H.;

MARIA m. J. Bagley, of Thornton, N. H.;

ANNA m. John Robinson, of Sanbornton, N. H.

CHILDREN OF TRUEWORTHY, (25) SON OF TRUE-WORTHY, (9) *Son of Stephen,* (3)

TRUEWORTHY, (56½) b.　, at ——, d.　, at Meredith, N. H.;

SAMUEL, b.　, at ——, d.　, at　do.;

DOLLY, b.　, at ——, d.　, at　do.;

JOANNA, b.　, at ——, d.　, at　do.;

Marriage.

TRUEWORTHY m. Polly Gilman, dau. of John G.

CHILDREN OF JOHN, (26) SON OF JONATHAN, (11) *Son of Samuel 2d,* (4)

SARAH, b. May 1, 1770, at Brentwood, N. H., d.　, at B.;

---

* On the town records, it is written " Nov."

SUSANNAH, b. May 3, 1773, at Brentwood, d. Jan. 1, 1774, at B.

Marriage.

SARAH m. Francis Becket.

Sixth Generation in America.

CHILDREN OF SAMUEL, (27) SON OF JOHN, (12) *Son of Samuel,* (5)

JOSIAH, (57) b. August 26, 1772, at Brentwood, N. H.,
    l. A. D. 1848, at B.;
JUDITH, b.   , at Brentwood, d.   , at B.;
ELIZABETH, b.   , at do.;
JOHN, b.   , at   do., d.   , at Skowhegan, Me.

Marriages.

JOSIAH m. 1st, Sarah Robinson; 2d, Sarah Robinson;
JUDITH m. Nathaniel Morrill;
ELIZABETH m. William Morrill;
JOHN m. Mary Clarkson.

CHILDREN OF JOHN, (28) SON OF JOHN, (12) *Son of Samuel,* (5)

JEREMIAH, (58) b. Dec. 13, 1774, at Brentwood, N. H.,
    l. A. D. 1848, at Brentwood;
ANDREW, b. June 8, 1777, at Brentwood, l. 1848, at B.;

†ELIZABETH, b. Feb. 1778, at Brentwood, l. 1848, at B.;

SAMUEL, b. Dec. 2, 1789, at Brentwood, d. July 3, 1839,
    at B.

Marriages.

HON. JEREMIAH m. Elizabeth Dudley, dau. of Samuel D.,
    June 18, 1810;

HON. ANDREW m. Mary Dudley, dau. of Josiah D.;

SAMUEL m. Dorothy Morrill.

CHILDREN OF WINTHROP, (29) SON OF JOHN, (12)
Son of Samuel, (5)

JOHN S., (59) b. July 2, 1780, at Brentwood, N. H., d.
    June 28, 1830, at Brentwood;

†SARAH, b. Nov. 29, 1782, at Brentwood, l. A. D. 1848,
    at B.

Marriage.

HON. JOHN S. m. Catharine Smith, dau. of ~~James S.~~

CHILDREN OF JOSIAH, (30) SON OF SAMUEL, (13)
Son of Samuel, (5)

MARY, b.   , at Brentwood, N. H., l. A. D. 1848, at B.;

ANN, b.   , at Brentwood, l. 1848, at Portsmouth, N. H.;

†JOSIAH, b.   , at Brentwood, d.   , at B.;

SAMUEL, b.   , at   do.,   l. A. D. 1848, at B.

Marriages.

MARY m. Hon. Andrew Dudley, son of John D. ;

ANN m. Simon Smith, of Portsmouth, N. H. ;

SAMUEL m. Mary Flint.

CHILDREN OF SAMUEL, (31) SON OF SAMUEL, (13)
Son of Samuel, (5)

DEBORAH G., b. March 23, 1777, at Brentwood, N. H.,
     l. 1848, at ——— ;

ELIZABETH, b. Jan. 30, 1779, at Brentwood, l.   , at B. ;

LEAVITT, b. Aug. 14, 1781, at Brentwood, d. Aug. 13,
     1827, at B.

Marriages.

DEBORAH G. m. Jonathan Robins ;

ELIZABETH m. Hon. Jeremiah Dudley, son of John D.,
     June 18, 1810.

CHILDREN OF JEREMY, (31¼) SON OF SAMUEL
P., (13¼) *Son of Stephen,* (6)

‡SAMUEL P., b.   , at New Hampton, N. H., d. about
     1838, at Salem, Mass.

Two daughters, names unknown.

CHILDREN OF HUBBARD, (31½) SON OF SAMUEL
P., (13½) *Son of Stephen,* (6)

SAMUEL, b. Oct. 26, 1789, at New Hampton, N. H.,
     l. 1848, at Portsmouth, N. H. ;

TIMOTHY, b. Aug. 26, 1792, at New Hampton, l. A. D.
1848;

HANNAH, b. June 23, 1795, at New Hampton, d. Oct.
1834, at St. Armanda, Canada E.;

SALLY, b. June 3, 1798, at New Hampton, l. A. D.
1848;

PETER, b. Aug. 22, 1801, at New Hampton, l. at Concord, N, H., A. D. 1848;

MOSES L., b. Nov. 20, 1803, at New Hampton, l. at Durham, C. E., A. D. 1848;

ELMIRA, b. Jan. 28, 1810, at New Hampton, d. at ——,
July 17, 1826.

Marriages.

DR. SAMUEL m. Susan D. Salisbury;

TIMOTHY m. 1st, Susan Fellows, March 23, 1815, who
died, Feb. 9, 1833; 2d, Mrs. Sarah Rowell, Oct.
12, 1833;

HANNAH m. Robert Aitkin, Jr., of St. Armanda, C. E.,
A. D. 1828;

PETER m. Eliza Bassett, of Derry, N. H.;

MOSES L. m. Hannah Stickney, of St. Armanda, 1829.

CHILDREN OF STEPHEN, (32) SON OF DAVIDSON, (14)
Son of Stephen, (6)

BETSEY, b.   , at ——, N. H.

Several others, names not known.

CHILDREN OF TIMOTHY, (33) Son of David-
son, (14) *Son of Stephen,* (6)

STEPHEN,* b.   , at Brentwood, N. H., d.   , at ——,
in the Revolutionary army;

TIMOTHY,*(61)*   , at ——, N. H., l. A. D. 1848, at ——;

LEVI,§ (60) b.   , at ——, do., d.   , at Vershire, Vt.;

SARAH, b.   , at ——,   do., l. A. D. 1848, at ——;

~~Jonas G., (61) b.   , at ——, N. H., l. A. D. 1848, at
New York City.~~

Marriage.

STEPHEN m. Deborah Elkins, of New Durham, N. H.;

LEVI m. Betsey Laroy, of Barnard, Vt.;

JONAS G. m. Mercy Strong;

SARAH m. Elijah Hawkins, of Meredith, N. H.

CHILDREN OF PETER C., (34) Son of Davidson, (14)
Son of Stephen, (6)

DAVID, b.   , at Brentwood, N. H.;

BENJAMIN, b.   , at do.;

STEPHEN, b.   , at do.;

BETSEY, b.   , at do.;

SUSAN, b.   , at do.;

MARY, b.   , at do.;

JERUSHA, b.   , at do.;

---

* Stephen left nine children, names unknown.

§ Levi had a family of twelve children, names unknown.

Marriages.

BETSEY m. Mr. Judkins, of York Co., Me.;
SUSAN m. Stephen Sleeper;
MARY m. James Marshall;
JERUSHA m. Mr. A. Clark.

CHILDREN OF JOHN, (35) SON OF STEPHEN, (15)
Son of Stephen, (6)

HANNAH, b.	, at	, N. H.;
SARAH, b.	, at	, do.;
JOHN, b.	, at	, do.;
ANN, b.	, at	, do.;
NATHANIEL, b.	, at	, do.;
MARY L., b.	, at	, do.

CHILDREN OF SAMUEL, (36) SON OF STEPHEN, (15)
Son of Stephen, (6)

| SAMUEL, b. | , at | , N. H; |
| ABEL, b. | , at | , do. |

CHILDREN OF PETER, (37) SON OF STEPHEN, (15)
Son of Stephen, (6)

ANNA, b.	, at Gilmanton, N. H.;
HANNAH, b.	, at do.;
PETER, b.	, at do.;
SUSAN, b.	, at do.;
NICHOLAS G., b.	, at do.;

CHILDREN OF JAMES, (38) Son of James, (17)
Son of James, (7)

DAVID;
JONATHAN; ⎫
JAMES; ⎬ This family is believed to have settled in
SARAH; ⎭ Canada East, near Lake Memphremagog.
DEBORAH.

THE SON OF STEPHEN, (39) Son of James, (17)
Son of James, (7)

ELIPHALET, (62) b. , at , N. H., d. , at Readfield, Me.

CHILDREN OF DANIEL, (40) Son of Samuel, (18)
Son of James, (7)

DANIEL, b. 1779, at , l. A. D. 1848, at , Ohio;
THOMAS, (62½) b. April 18, 1783, at , l. 1848, at
Pittsfield, Me.;
MOSES, b. , 1786, at , l. 1848, at , Ohio;
SAMUEL, b. , 1788, at , l. do. at , do.;
DAVID, b. , 1790, at , l. do. at , do.;
MARY, b. , 1777, at , l. do. at Fayette, Me.;
†SUSANNA, b. , 1781, at , l. do. at do. ;
MEHITABLE, b. , at , d. 1833, at .

Marriages.

REV. THOMAS m. Anna Reant, of Farmington, Me., Jan-
uary 3, 1809, who was b. Jan. 6, 1787;
MARY m. Mr. Judkins;
MEHITABLE m. Mr. Jacobs.

CHILDREN OF SAMUEL, (41) Son of Samuel, (18)
Son of James, (7)

SAMUEL,
AARON,
JAMES.
} This family, if living, probably reside in some part of the State of Ohio.

CHILDREN OF MICAJAH, (42) Son of Samuel, (18)
Son of James, (7)

JOHN,
SAMUEL,
SUSANNA.
} This family is believed to have settled in Kennebec County, Me., and some of them in the *town* of Sidney, in that County.

CHILDREN OF JEREMIAH, (43) Son of Samuel, (18)
Son of James, (7)

JEREMIAH, b.   , at   , Me. or N. H.;
BENJAMIN F., b.   , at   ,   do.;
REV. DAVID, b.   , at   ,   do. l. A. D. 1848,
    at Ann Arbor, Mich.;
JOHN, b.   , at   , Me. l. 1848, at Bath, N. Y.;
MOSES, b.   , at   , l.   , at   "
THOMAS J., b.   , at   , l.   , at Buffalo, N. Y.;
Several daughters, whose names are unknown to me.

CHILDREN OF MOSES, (44) Son of Samuel, (18)
Son of James, (7)

PETER, b. A. D. 1777, at   , d. A. D. 1819, at   ;
MOSES, (63) b. A. D. 1778, at   , d. A. D. 1842, at
    Mainesville, Ohio;

John, b. A. D. 1784, at   , d. A. D.   , at   ;
Daniel, b. do. 1782, at   , d. do. 1819, at   ;
Sleeper, b. do. 1789, at   , d. do.   , at   ;
Apphia, b. do. 1787, at   , l. do. 1848, at Cincin-
 nati, Ohio;
Mehitable, b. A. D. 1791, at   , l. 1848, at   ,
 Marion Co., Ohio.

Marriage.

Mehitable m. Mr. Fisher, of   , Marion Co., Ohio.

CHILDREN OF ELIPHALET, (45) Son of Sam-uel, (18) *Son of James,* (7)

Jonathan, b. at , d. 1814, Portland, Me.,
Gilman,   in the army.
James,
John,   This family emigrated to West Virginia,
Joanna, where some of them are probably yet
Mary,   living. The town and county in which
Hannah, they settled are unknown to me.
Deborah,

Marriages.

Mary m. Mr. Gibbs;
Deborah m. Mr. Gray.

CHILDREN OF JAMES, (46) Son of Samuel, (18) *Son of James,* (7)

Elias, b.   , at   ;
Several others, whose names are unknown to me.

CHILDREN OF JOHN 2d, (47) Son of John, (19) *Son of James,* (7)

James, (64) b. Sept. 16, 1782, at   , l. A. D. 1848, at Norridgewock, Me. ;

Caleb, b. Apr. 8, 1779, at   , d.   , at Mt. Vernon, Me.;

Gilman, (65) b. Mar. 8, 1788, at   , l. 1848, at Kingfield, Me.;

Eliza, b. Dec. 1791, at Mt. Vernon, Me., l. 1848, at do.;

John, b. July 3, 1773, at   , d. Nov. 1828, at   , Me.

Marriages.

James m. Sarah Nickerson, A. D. 1804;

Caleb m. Miss Gilman ;

Capt. Gilman m. 1st, Miss Gilman ; 2d. Miriam S. Dudley, dau. of Hon. Nathl. D.;

Eliza m. Ebenezer Pilsbury ;

John m. Miss Gilman.

CHILDREN OF JAMES, (48) Son of John, (19) *Son of James,* (7)

†Elizabeth, b. Oct. 20, 1795, at Raymond, N. H., l. A. D. 1848, at Poplin, N. H.;

Mary, b. Aug. 7, 1791, at Raymond, d. 1835, at R.

†James, b. Mar. 8, 1799, at do. d. Aug. 23, 1837, at do.;

John, b. July 20, 1800, at do. l. 1848, at Portsmouth;

Moses, b. May 29, 1803, at do. l. do. at Raymond;

†Susanna, b. Feb. 11, 1806, at do. l. do. at Boston, Mass.

Marriages.

MARY m. Abijah Lovering, of Chester, N. H.;

JOHN m. Mary Robie, dau. of John R., of Candia, N. H.;

MOSES m. Mary A. Hunt, of Sandown, N. H.

CHILDREN OF NATHANIEL, (49) SON OF JOHN, (19)
Son of James, (7)

EDMUND, (66) b. Oct. 4, 1784, at Raymond, N. H.,
d. March 25, 1835, at Oxford, Ohio;

NATHANIEL, (67) b. March 26, 1789, at Mt. Vernon, Me.,
d. June 4, 1790, at Mt. V.;

JOHN, b. Nov. 19, 1798, at do. d. Oct. 5, 1800, at Mt. V.;

NATHANIEL, 2d, b. Aug. 13, 1799, at Mt. Vernon, l. 1848,
at   , Virginia;

JOHN G., (68) b. May 4, 1806, at Mt. Vernon, l. 1848, at
Kingfield, Me.;

WILLIAM K., (69) b. Nov. 4, 1810, at Kingfield, l. 1848,
at Kingfield, Me.;

BETSEY, b. Jan. 19, 1786, at Raymond, N. H., l. 1848,
at Mt. Vernon, Me.;

MARY, b. Aug. 10, 1787, at Raymond, d. Jan. 3, 1790;

NANCY, b. Nov. 15, 1790, at Mt. Vernon, l. 1848, at
Kingfield, Me.;

POLLY, b. Mar. 15, 1792, at Mt. Vernon, d. April 3, 1793,
at the same town;

‡IRENIA, b. Sept. 28, 1793, at Mt. Vernon, d. Nov.   ,
1812, at Kingfield, Me.;

SALLY, b. June 12, 1796, at Mt. Vernon, d. Feb. 1839,
at Freeman, Me.;

MARY, 2d, b. Sept. 26, 1801, at Mt. Vernon, d. Nov. 16,
   at Kingfield, Me.;

MIRIAM S., b. Feb. 1, 1803, at Mt. V., l. 1848, at K.

Marriages.

EDMUND m. Rebecca Bangs, dau. of Capt. Dean B.,
   of Sidney, Me., Nov. 29, 1806;

NATHANIEL 2d, m. 1st, ———; 2d, Sally Stiles;

JOHN G. ESQ., m. Thirza Smith, A. D. 1830;

WILLIAM K. m. Harriet B. Pulling, dau. of George P.;

BETSEY m. Thomas Atkins of Mt. Vernon, Me.;

NANCY m. Spencer Gilbert;

SALLY m. Capt. Alexander Blanchard;

MIRIAM S. m. Capt. Gilman Dudley, son of Capt. John D.;

‡IRENIA m. Joseph Moody.

CHILDREN OF MOSES, (50) SON OF JOHN, (19)
   Son of James, (7)

JOHN, (70) b. Oct. 3, 1789, at Raymond, N. H., l. A. D.
   1848, at Waite, Me.;

GILMAN, (71) b. Dec. 28, 1790, at Raymond, d. Feb. 4,
   1835, at Raymond;

MOSES, (72) b. Sept. 10, 1792, at Raymond, l. A. D. 1848,
   at   , Coles Co., Ill.;

JAMES, (73) b. Feb. 10, 1794, at Raymond, l. 1848, at
   Roxbury, Mass.;

GUILFORD, (74) b. Dec. 7, 1795, at Raymond, l. 1848, at
   Coles Co., Ill.;

FRANKLIN, (75) b. Nov. 7, 1799, at Raymond, l. 1848, at
   Raymond;

ELBRIDGE G., b. Aug. 13, 1811, at Raymond, l. 1848, at
    Boston, Mass.;

BETSEY, b. Sept. 12, 1788, at Raymond, l. 1848, at Deer-
    field, N. H.;

SALLY, b. Oct. 17, 1797, at Raymond, l. 1848, at R.;

NANCY, b. July 9, 1805, at   do.   l. 1848, at do.

Marriages.

JOHN, ESQ., m. Miss S. Sweat, of Maine;

CAPT. GILMAN m. Mary Bean, dau. of Nathan Bean, of
    Candia, N. H.;

MOSES m. Mrs. Mary Henry;

JAMES m. Mrs. Abby Brown, who died Sept. 14, 1843,
    aged 35 years;

GUILFORD m. Mary Wiley;

FRANKLIN m. Olive Bean, dau. of Nathan B.;

ELBRIDGE G., ESQ., m. Miss C. Duncan, dau. of Isaac D.;

BETSEY m. REV. Peter Philbrick, of Deerfield;

SALLY m. Mr. Barnard Tucker, of Raymond;

NANCY m. Gen. Henry Tucker, of   do.

CHILDREN OF JOSEPH, (51) SON OF JOSEPH, (20)
    Son of James, (7)

BENJAMIN, (75½) b. Oct. 25, 1776, at Raymond, N. H.,
    l. A. D. 1848, at Mt. Vernon, Me.;

JOSEPH, b. Feb. 7, 1790, at Raymond, l. 1848, at R.;

SAMUEL, b. May 5, 1796, at R., l. 1848, at Candia, N. H.;

STEPHEN, b. July 27, 1798, at Raymond, l. 1848, at Buffalo, N. Y.;

HANNAH, b. Sept. 17, 1778, at Raymond, d. May 26, 1835, at Raymond;

Twins { DEBORAH, b. July 17, 1780, at Readfield, d. Oct. 20, 1815, at Raymond;

SUSANNA, b. July 17, 1780, at Readfield, d. Mar. 25, 1806, at Raymond;

†MARY, b. July 27, 1783, at Raymond, l. 1848, at R.;

†EUNICE, b. Sept. 20, 1787, at do. d. July 1, 1842, at R.;

Marriages.

BENJAMIN m. 1st, Elizabeth Smith; 2d, Mrs. Sarah Tucker;

JOSEPH, ESQ., m. Sally Dudley, dau. of Thomas D.;

SAMUEL m. 1st, Miss Pillsbury; 2d,   ;

STEPHEN m. Hannah Turner;

HANNAH m. Mr. J. Fullington;

DEBORAH m. Mr. J. Hook;

SUSANNA m. Samuel Tilton.

CHILDREN OF THOMAS, (52) SON OF JOSEPH, (20) *Son of James*, (7)

†JOHN, b. Nov. 6, 1800, at Raymond, N. H., l. 1848, at Danville, Iowa T.;

†THOMAS J., (76) b. Jan. 13, 1803, at Raymond, d. Jan. 19, 1835, at Raymond;

7

†Esther, b. Mar. 22, 1807, at Raymond, d. Oct. 13, 1838,
    at Raymond ;

‡Francis D., b. Feb. 4, 1809, at Raymond, d. Oct.   ,
    1829, upon the Mississippi River ;

David M., (76½) b. Dec. 25, 1811, at Raymond, l. A. D.
    1848, at Danville, Iowa T. ;

Sally, b. Mar. 6, 1795, at Raymond, l. 1848, at R. ;

‡Mary, b. May 23, 1797, at R., l. do. at Boston ;

‡Asenath, b. Mar. 10, 1799, at R., l. do. at do. ;

‡Susanna, b. Mar. 3, 1805, at R., l. do. at Chester.

Marriages.

Francis D. m. Miss Palmer, of Cincinnati, Ohio ;

David M. m. Sarah Proctor ;

Sally m. Joseph Dudley, Esq., son of Joseph D. ;

Mary m. Joseph Jenness, of Epping, N. H. ;

Asenath m. Andrew Johnson, of Lynn, Mass. ;

Susanna m. John Locke, Esq.   .

CHILDREN OF TRUEWORTHY, (53) Son of BILEY, (21) *Son of Nicholas,* (8)

John, b.   , at Brentwood, N. H.,   ;

Benjamin, b. Aug. 18, 1785, at Newbury, N. H.,   ;

Jonathan, b. Feb. 4, 1787, at N., d. Apr. 10, 1795, at N. ;

Trueworthy, (77) b. July 21, 1793, at N.   ;

Alice, b. April 27, 1796, at N.   ;

Ephraim, b. Oct. 24, 1799, at N.   ;

WILLIAM C., (78) b. Aug. 13, 1801, at Newbury, N. H.;
SALLY, b. April 13, 1807, at   do.   .

Marriages.

TRUEWORTHY m. Mary Chase, Nov. 16, 1820, at New-
    bury, N. H.;
WILLIAM C. m. Nancy ———.

CHILDREN OF TRUEWORTHY, (54) SON OF JOSEPH, (23) *Son of Nicholas,* (8)

NICHOLAS, b.	, d.	, at sea;	
JOSEPH, b.	, 1785,		;
HANNAH, b.	, 1787,		;
ABIJAH, b.	, 1789,		;
BENJAMIN, b.	, 1792,		;
MARTHA, b.	, 1790,		;
ABIGAIL, b.	, 1789, d.	, 1806,	;
TRUEWORTHY, b.	, 1801,		;
THOMAS, b.	, 1803,		;
WILLIAM, b.	, 1804,		;
SAMUEL, b.	, 1806,		.

Marriages.

JOSEPH m. Mrs. Brooks, 1814;
HANNAH m. Robert Savage, merchant, of Portland, Me.;
ABIJAH m. Betsey Folsom, 1816;
BENJAMIN m. Clarissa Sibley, 1817;
MARTHA m. Benjamin Briggs, 1816;
THOMAS m. 1st, Clarissa Perry; 2d, Sally Carpenter.

CHILDREN OF TRUEWORTHY, (55) Son of Gilman, (24) *Son of Trueworthy,* (9)

By first wife.

SALLY, b.   at Pembroke, l. 1848, at Conway, N. H.;

POLLY, b.   at P. l. 1848, at P.;

Two others, died in infancy;

Children by the second wife.

COGSWELL, (78¼) b. April, 1792, at P., l. 1848, at P.;

‡RICE, b. April, 1794, at Pembroke, l. 1848, at P.;

TRUEWORTHY, (79) b. Sept. 13, 1796, at Pembroke, l. 1848, at Boston, Mass.;

GILMAN, (79¼) b. 1798, at P., l. 1848, at N. Y. city;

JAMES H., (79½) b. 1801, at P., l. 1848, at Boston;

‡BENJ. F., b.   at P., l. 1848, at Milton, Mass.;

†HAMILTON, b.   at P., l. 1848, at N. Y. city;

ELIZABETH J., b.   at Pembroke, l. 1848, at Milton, Mass.

Marriages.

SALLY m. John Knox, of Conway, N. H.;

POLLY m. Andrew Gault, of Pembroke;

COGSWELL m. Nancy True, dau. of Benjamin T., of Deerfield, N. H.;

RICE m. Nancy H. Sargent, dau. of Dr. S., of Chester;

TRUEWORTHY, trader, m. Mary Fisk, dau. of Benjamin F., of Pembroke;

GILMAN, trader, m. Margaret Cochran, dau. of Thomas C., son of John C., of Pembroke;

JAMES H. m. 1st, Betsey Eaton, dau. of Dr. Thomas E., of Francestown, N. H.; 2d, Mrs. Elizabeth C. Hoyt, of Dover, N. H.;

BENJAMIN F. m. Mary E. Littlefield, dau. of Samuel L., of Milton, Mass.;

ELIZABETH J. m. Mr. R. P. Fenno, of Milton, Mass.

CHILDREN OF SAMUEL C., (56) SON OF GILMAN, (24).
Son of Trueworthy, (9)

NANCY, b. Feb. 11, 1791, at Sanbornton, N. H.;

JOHN, (80) b. March 30, 1793, at S.   l. 1848, at Holderness, N. H.;

SALLY, b. April 1, 1795, at Sanbornton, l. 1848, at S.;

MARY, b. Aug. 4, 1797, at   do. l. 1848, at Thornton;

MERCY, b. Dec. 9, 1799, at   do.   d. Sept. 8, 1825;

ABIGAIL, b. May 13, 1802, at   do.   l. 1848,   ;

HANNAH, b. Sept. 19, 1804, at do.   l. do. at   ;

ELIZA, b. June 16, 1807, at   do.   l. do. at   ;

LUCIA, b. Aug. 3, 1809, at   do.   l. do. at   .

Marriages.

NANCY m. John Lang, Sept. 1, 1831, at New Hampton;

JOHN m. Sally Prescott, of Holderness, N. H., Apr. 2, 1827;

SALLY m. Thomas Shute, of Bethlehem, Feb. 21,* 1844;

MARY m. Benj. Shute, of Sanbornton, Nov. 2, 1830;

ABIGAIL m. John S. Lane, Esq., May 12, 1829;

HANNAH m. Smith Marston, of Parsonsfield, Me., June 9, 1824;

ELIZA m. Daniel M. Huse, Esq., Nov. 25, 1830;

LUCIA m. Joseph W. Blake, of New Hampton, April 25, 1839.

---

* The town record is "February 24th."

Seventh Generation in America.

CHILDREN OF JOSIAH, (57) Son of Samuel, (27)
Son of John, (12)

†Sarah, b. June 20, 1797, at Brentwood,* N. H.,
   d. Feb. 6, 1840, at Brentwood;

†Josiah R., b. Oct. 1, 1802, at Brentwood, d. Aug. 23,
   1832, at Brentwood, N. H.

John W., b. Nov. 1, 1829, at Brentwood, l. 1848, at B.

CHILDREN OF JEREMIAH, (58) Son of John, (28)
Son of John, (12)

Joanna, b. Aug. 18, 1811, at Brentwood, N. H., l. A. D.
   1848, at East Kingston, N. H.;

†Mary L., b. June 21, 1813, at Brentwood, l. 1848, at B.;

†Sarah E., b. Apr. 22, 1814, at   do.   l. do.,   at B.;

Deborah, b. May 1, 1817, at   do.   l. do.,   at B.;

†Jeremiah, b. Nov. 13, 1819, at   do.   l. do.,   at B.

Marriages.

Joanna m. John Tilton;

Deborah m. Mr. J. Robinson.

CHILDREN OF JOHN S., (59) Son of Winthrop, (29)
Son of John, (12)

Hannah, b. Nov. 18, 1813, at Brentwood, N. H., l. 1848,
   at Plymouth, N. H.;

---

* Brentwood was detached from Exeter, A. D. 1742, and Epping
was detached from E., 1741.

WINTHROP H., b. Apr. 1, 1816, at Brentwood, l. 1848, at B.;
SARAH, b. June, 1820, at B., l. 1848, at Epping, N. H.;
CATHARINE, b. 1818, at B., d. July 26, 1820, at B;
†CATHARINE, 2d. b. May 9, 1822, at B., l. 1848.

Marriages.

HANNAH m. Arthur Ward, of Plymouth, N. H.;
CAPT. WINTHROP H. m. Frances Robinson;
SARAH m. John W. Morril, of Epping, N. H.

CHILDREN OF TIMOTHY, (59½) SON OF HUB-BARD, (31½) *Son of Samuel P.*, (13½)

SUSAN, b. Feb. 10, 1816;
MARY J., b. March 4, 1819;
TIMOTHY F., b. May 1, 1821, d. Nov. 22, 1822;
MOSES W., b. Nov. 25, 1823;
NANCY, b. Aug. 31, 1827;
PETER F., b. Jan. 8, 1830;
LAURA A., b. Aug. 21, 1833.

Marriages.

SUSAN m. James Gage, March 23, 1834;
MARY JANE m. George F. Roberts, Nov. 24, 1842;
NANCY m. Morah Scott, Jan. 9, 1846.

CHILDREN OF LEVI, (60) SON OF TIMOTHY, (33) *Son of Davidson*, (14)

This family consisted of twelve children, all of whose names are unknown to me.

CHILDREN OF TIMOTHY (61) Son of Timothy, (33)
Son of Davidson, (14)

Cyrus, b.   , at   , l. 1848, at   ;
Hiram,* b.   , at   , l. do. in Illinois ;
Timothy,§ b.   , at   , l. do.   ;
Jonas G., b.   , at   , l. do. in New York city.

Marriages.

Cyrus m. Abigail Amsden ;
Hiram m. Miss Johnson ;
Timothy m. Almira Blanchard, of Barre, Vt. ;
Jonas G. m. Augusta Aikens, dau. of Hon. Asa A., of
 Windsor, Vt.

CHILDREN OF ELIPHALET, (62) Son of Ste-
phen, (39) Son of James, (17)

Elizabeth, b. Jan. 1, 1782, at Readfield, Me., l. 1848, at R. ;
Samuel,(81) b. Feb. 11, 1785, at do. d. Nov. 25, 1835, at R.;
Stephen, (81½) b. July, 1788, at do. l. 1848, at R. ;
John, (82) b. Aug. 28, 1790, at do. l. do., at R. ;
Prudence, b. July, 1792, at   do. l. do. at   ;
Henry, (83) b. Aug. 16, 1795, at R., l. 1848, at R. ;
Nancy, b. Dec. 26, 1798, at R., l. 1848, at R. ;
David, b. Oct. 11, 1806, at do. l. do. at Boston, Mass. ;
†Mehitable, b. 1808, at R., l. 1848, at   do.

---

* Three children of his family were born in Illinois.
§ Of his family of nine children only three are now living.

SEVENTH GENERATION. **61**

Marriages.

SAMUEL m. Mary Childs, of Hallowell, Me.;

ELIZABETH m. Currier Brown, of Readfield;

STEPHEN m. Sibbil Simpson, of Clinton;

JOHN m. Polly Brown, of Readfield;

PRUDENCE m. Mr. Moore;

HENRY m. Dolly Maxfield, of Mt. Vernon;

NANCY m. Daniel Ingraham, of   do.;

DAVID m. Thankful B. King, of Boston, Mass.

CHILDREN OF THOMAS, (62½) SON OF DANIEL, (40)
Son of Samuel, (18)

Born at Readfield, Me.

SUSAN, b. March 25, 1810, lives at Gardiner, Me.;

SARAH, b. March 1, 1812, lives at Cincinnati, Ohio;

DANIEL, b. Feb. 17, 1814, lives at Alexandria, do.

DAVID, b. Sept. 26, 1818, lives at Oldtown, Me.;

ABIGAIL A., b. May 13, 1821, lives at Fairfield, Me.;

JOSEPH, b. Jan. 28, 1828, lives at   do.

Marriages.

SUSAN m. Capt. George Green, Aug. 1837;

SARAH m. James Clough, of Readfield, Me., Feb. 1835;

DANIEL m. —— ——, Sept. 1842;

DAVID m. —— ——, Sept. 1846;

ABIGAIL A. m. Samuel Webb, of Pittsfield, Jan. 2, 1842.

CHILDREN OF MOSES, (63) SON OF MOSES, (44)
Son of Samuel, (18)

SILAS, b.   1800,   l. 1848, at Mainesville, Ohio;

MARY, b.   1803,   l. do. in Ohio;

8

SIBBIL, b.   1805,   l. 1848, in Ohio ;
MEHITABLE, b.   1808,   l. do. in do. ;
DANIEL, b.   1810,   l. do. in do. ;
EMILY, b.   1812,   l. do. in do. ;
MOSES S., b.   1814,   l. do. in do.

CHILDREN OF JAMES, (64) SON OF JOHN, (47)
Son of John, (19)

ALVIN, b. June 8, 1805, at Mt. Vernon, Me., l. 1848, at
    Lowell, Mass. ;
ALMIRA, b. April 14, 1807, at Mt. Vernon ;

All born at Norridgewock, Me.

ELIZA, b. April 12, 1809 ;
SARAH, b. June 16, 1811 ;
ROSILLA, b. Feb. 28, 1814 ;
JAMES L., b. March 22, 1816 ;
LUCINDA, b. Sept. 9, 1818 ;
MERCY A., b. July 16, 1820, d. May 17, 1844 ;
CAROLINE F., b. Dec. 22, 1823 ;
ALBION K. P., b. Feb. 10, 1825, d. Aug. 10, 1826 ;
MARY A., b. Aug. 6, 1827 ;
HARRIET M., b. Nov. 26, 1829.

CHILDREN OF GILMAN, (65) SON OF JOHN, (47)
Son of John, (19)

By the first wife.

HANNAH, b.   , at   , Me. ;
HENRY, b.   , at   , do. d. at Kingfield ;
HIRAM, b.   , at   , do. d. at Gardiner ;
JOHN, b.   , at   , do. ;

Susan, b.	, at Kingfield;
Cyrus, b.	, at do.;
Ward S., b.	, at do.;
Gilman, b.	, at do.;
Eveline, b.	, at do.;
Elizabeth, b.	, at do.;

By the second wife.

CHILDREN OF EDMUND, (66) Son of Nathaniel, (49) *Son of John,* (19)

Laura A., b. Nov. 11, 1807, at Mt. Vernon, Me., l. 1848, at Canaan, Me.;

Elkanah B., b. May 22, 1809, at Sidney, Me., l. do. at Freeman, Me.;

Harrison, b. Oct. 9, 1811, at Sidney, d. Jan. 4, 1816, at Kingfield, Me.;

Julia O., b. April 11, 1815, l. 1848, at Salem, Mass.;
Albion S., b. Aug. 6, 1816, l. do. at Dedham, do.;
Eunice S., b. Aug. 15, 1818, l. do. at Salem, do.;
Mary L., b. Aug. 4, 1820, l. do. in Wisconsin;
Dean, b. May 23, 1823, l. do. at Cambridge;
Rebecca B., b. Dec. 16, 1825, l. do. at Salem, Mass.

Born at Kingfield, Me.

Marriages.

Laura A. m. Sylvanus F. Jewell, of Canaan, Me.;
Elkanah B., farmer, m. Harriet Fessenden;
Julia O. m. Joseph A. Paine, of Salem, Mass.;
Albion S., dentist, m. Lydia F. Manley, dau. of Amasa M.;
Mary L. m. Michael E. Ames, Esq.

CHILDREN OF NATHANIEL, (67) Son of Nathaniel, (49) *Son of John,* (19)

Julius A., b. in Virginia;
Several others, doubtless, whose names are unknown.

CHILDREN OF JOHN G., (68) Son of Nathaniel, (49) *Son of John,* (19)

Elvira, b.   , at Freeman, Me., d.   , at   , Me.;
Nathaniel, b.   , at   do.;
Thirza, b.   , at   do.;
Several others, whose names are unknown.

CHILDREN OF WILLIAM K., (69) Son of Nathaniel, (49) *Son of John,* (19)

Ann S., b.   , at Kingfield, Me.;
Harriet G., b.   , at   do.;
Llewellen, b.   , at   do.;
Several others, names unknown.

CHILDREN OF JOHN, (70) Son of Moses, (50) *Son of John,* (19)

Eliza, b.   , at   , Me.;
Nancy, b.   , at   , do.;
Lydia A., b.   , at   , do.;
Sarah, b.   , at   , do.;
Andrew J., b.   , at   , do.;
John, b.   , at   , do.

CHILDREN OF GILMAN, (71) Son of Moses, (50)
Son of John, (19)

Born at Raymond, N. H.

HANNAH B., b. May 11, 1816, l. 1848, at Raymond;

PARTHENIA A., b. May 12, 1818, l. do. at Boston, Ms.;

JOHN G., b. Sept. 2, 1821, l. 1848, at Slatersville, R. I.;

NANCY G., b. Apr. 4, 1824, l. do. at Raymond;

MARY E., b. Sept. 18, 1827, l. do. at   do.;

EMILY B., b. Feb. 4, 1830, l. do. at   do.;

SARAH G., b. Sept. 10, 1832, l. do. at   do.;

Marriage.

JOHN G. m. Harriet Sulliway, of Stoughton, Mass., Sept. 15, 1844;

THE DAUGHTER OF MOSES, (72) Son of Moses, (50)
Son of John, (19)

VIRGINIA, b. 1837, at Coles Co., Ill., l. 1848, at C. Co.

THE DAUGHTER OF JAMES, (73) Son of Moses, (50)
Son of John, (19)

MAHALA, b. July 15, 1836, at Coles Co., l. 1848.

CHILDREN OF GUILFORD, (74) Son of Moses, (50)
Son of John, (19)

FLORENCE, b. 1831; HANNAH, b. July 29, 1836; JAMES, d.; JOHN; ELI; ELIZABETH; NANCY;—all born in Coles Co. Illinois.

CHILDREN OF FRANKLIN, (75) Son of Moses, (50)
Son of John, (19)

Born at Raymond, N. H.

FRANKLIN B., b. May 23, 1827, l. 1848, at Boston ;

Moses G., b. Aug. 12, 1828,   l. do. at Raymond ;

OLIVE E., b. Aug. 13, 1831,   l. do. at   do. ;

NANCY G., b. Jan. 21, 1834,   l. do. at   do. ;

MARGERY R., b. Jan. 17, 1836, d. Oct., 1842, at do. ;

CAROLINE O., b. Sept. 8, 1838, d. do. 10, do. at do. ;

AUGUSTUS R., b. June 2, 1830, d. do. 27, do. at do. ;

CHILDREN OF BENJAMIN, (75½) Son of Joseph, (51)
Son of Joseph, (20)

JAMES, (84) ; SALLY ; THOMAS J. ; POLLY ; †JOSEPH ; SAMUEL ; BENJAMIN ; JESSE, and JOHN ;—all born at Mt. Vernon, Me.

Marriages.

JAMES m. Lucinda Whittier ;

SALLY m. Elias Sherburne ;

THOMAS J. m. Lorinda Fifield ;

POLLY m. James Neale ;

SAMUEL m. Miss Currier ;

JOHN m. Miss Staine.

CHILDREN OF THOMAS J., (76) Son of Thomas, (52)
Son of Joseph, (20)

MARY E., b. May 31, 1827, at Readfield, Me. ;

ALBIÓN K. P., b. July 15, 1829, at do. ;

Ellen F., b. Nov. 8, 1830, at Readfield, Me. ;
Benj. F., b. June 24, 1832, at   do. ;
Surana, b. May 7, 1834, at   do. ;
Octavia T., b. Mar. 22, 1835, at do. ;

CHILDREN OF DAVID M., (76½) Son of Thomas, (52)
Son of Joseph, (20)

A Daughter, b.   , at Cincinnati, Ohio, d.   1838, at C. ;
Florilla J., b.   , 1841, at C., l. 1848, at Danville,
    Iowa Territory.

CHILDREN OF TRUEWORTHY, (77) Son of Trueworthy, (53) Son of Biley, (21)

Jonathan C., b. Jan. 7, 1822, at Newbury, N. H.;
Winthrop C., b. Nov. 24, 1823, at   do;
Betsey A., b. Jan. 3, 1826, at   do.

CHILDREN OF WILLIAM C., (78) Son of Trueworthy, (53) Son of Biley, (21)

Orison, b. Feb. 28, 1822, at Newbury, N. H. ;
Mary Ann, b. Jan. 16, 1824, at do.
Lucretia, b. Sept. 15, 1825, at do. ;
Phebe, b. Dec. 18, 1827, at   do. ;
Alzira, b. July 10, 1830, at do. ;
Almira, b. July 19, 1836, at do.

CHILDREN OF COGSWELL, (78½) Son of Trueworthy, (55) Son of Gilman, (24)

Trueworthy; Elizabeth; Ann; Sarah; Mary;—all
    born at Pembroke, N. H.

CHILDREN OF TRUEWORTHY, (79) Son of True-worthy, (55) *Son of Gilman*, (24)

Born at Pembroke.

MARY FRANCES, b. Nov. 1, 1821, d. Feb. 16, 1828, at Pembroke, N. H.;

SARAH E., b. Jan. 3, 1824, l. 1848, at Boston, Mass.;

AUGUSTA E., b. June 3, 1827, l. 1848, at Boston;

WARREN A., b. Nov. 19, 1829, d. Jan. 24, 1831, at B.;

JAMES F., b. Dec. 17, 1831, at Boston;

GEORGE B., b. May 4, 1834, at B., d. Aug. 7, 1834, at B.;

JOSEPHINE, b. July 1, 1835, at Dorchester, d. Jan. 6, 1836;

HARRIET F., b. Feb. 1, 1837, at D.;

MARY FRANKLIN, b. March 10, 1843, at Milton, Mass.

Marriage.

SARAH E. m. Joseph Baxter, of Boston, Dec. 21, 1847.

CHILDREN OF GILMAN, (79½) Son of True-worthy, (55) *Son of Gilman*, (24)

A son, b. at Penbroke, d. young;

THOMAS C., b. at P., l. 1848, at New York city;

ELIZABETH, b. at P., (?) d. young, at New Bedford, Mass.;

FRANCENA, b. at New Bedford, l. 1848, at N. Y. city;

A daughter, b. at N. B., d. young, at N. B.;

GILMAN, b. at N. Y. city, l. 1848, at N. Y.;

ORVILLE D., b. at N. Y., l. 1848, at N. Y.

CHILDREN OF JAMES H., (79½) Son of True-worthy, (55) *Son of Gilman*, (24)

THOMAS E., b. 1839, at Ware, N. H. l. at Boston, 1848;

A son, b. at Boston, d. in infancy ;
FRANKLIN H., b. Feb. 23, 1848, at Boston.

CHILDREN OF JOHN, (80) SON OF SAMUEL C., (56)
Son of Gilman, (24)

MERCY, b. Jan. 1828, at Holderness, N. H., l. 1848, at H. ;
MARY, b. 1830, at H., l. 1848, at H.

Eighth Generation in America.

CHILDREN OF SAMUEL, (81) SON OF ELIPHALET, (62)
Son of Stephen, (39)

MARGARET, b. Apr. 14, 1818, d. at Readfield, Me. ;
SOPHIA, b. Mar. 11, 1820, l. 1848, at Vassalboro', do. ;
JOHN C., b. Mar. 24, 1823, l. do. at Readfield ;
ATWOOD, b. July 26, 1824, l. do. at   do. ;
JONAS, b. Feb. 15, 1827, l.   do. at sea ;
BELINDA, b. Mar. 5, 1831, l. do. at Readfield ;

Born at Readfield, Me.

Marriage.

SOPHIA m. —— ——.

CHILDREN OF STEPHEN, (81½) SON OF ELIPH-
ALET, (62) *Son of Stephen,* (39)

HARRIET, b. at Readfield, Me., d. at R. ;
CATHARINE, b. at   do.   d. at Gardiner, Me. ;
WILLIAM, b. at   do. l. 1848 ;
GEORGE, b. at   do. l. at Cambridgeport, Ms., 1848 ;
MARTHA, b. at   do. l. at Readfield, 1848 ;
†PRUDENCE, b. at   do. l. at   do.   do.

9

Marriages.

WILLIAM m. Caroline Packard;
MARTHA m. Charles ———.

CHILDREN OF JOHN (82) SON OF ELIPHALET, (62)
Son of Stephen, (39)

Born at Readfield, Me.

EMILY, b. Jan. 17, 1819, l. at Readfield;
MEHITABLE, b. Nov. 7, 1820, l. at do;
CHARLES, b. May 27, 1823, l. at Farmington;
NELSON, b. Dec. 19, 1826, d.   , at Readfield;
GREENGROVE, b. Nov. 27, 1828, l. at   do.;
SERENA, b. Mar. 24, 1831,   l. at   do.;
ORRIN, b. Sept. 3, 1833,   l. at   do.;
MARTIN V. April 29, 1839,   l. at   do.;
DAVID, b.   l. at   do.;

Marriage.

CHARLES m. Miss Young.

CHILDREN OF HENRY, (83) SON OF ELIPHALET, (62)
Son of Stephen, (39)

Born at Readfield, Me.

HENRY H., b. March 26, 1816, d.   at Waltham, Ms.;
CAROLINE, b. Nov. 20, 1817, d. June 2, 1830, at R.;
MOSES S., b. June 12, 1819, l. A. D. 1848, at   do.;
MEHITABLE, b. May 15, 1821, l. do.   do.   at   do.;
THOMAS, b. May 18, 1823, d. Aug 24, 1829, at do.;
CHARLES S., b. Apr. 19, 1825, l. A. D. 1848, at do.;

Born at Readfield, Me.

JANE, b. June 12, 1827, d. Mar. 13, 1831 at R.;

LYDIA A., b. Aug. 4, 1830, l. A. D. 1848, at do.;

DAVID, b. Dec. 26, 1831, l. do. do. at do.;

JOHN, b. Nov. 14, 1834, l. do. do. at do.;

SILAS, b. l. do. do. at do.;

Marriages.

HENRY H. m. Miss Bartlett;

MOSES S. m. Electa —— ;

MEHITABLE m. James Clough.

CHILDREN OF JAMES, (84) SON OF BENJAMIN, (75½)
Son of Joseph, (51)

Born at Readfield, Me.

WILLIAM K., b. March 13, 1820;

GEORGE W., b. May, 1821;

JOHN S., b. April 13, 1823;

LUCINDA W., b. Dec. 18, 1824;

JOSEPH, b. Dec. 23, 1826;

JOSIAH, b. July 24, 1828;

JAMES H., b. June 11, 1831;

CHARLOTTE A., b. June 21, 1833;

MARY E., b. June 29, 1835.

ADDITIONS TO THE FOREGOING RECORDS.

A "THOMAS DUDLEY," mariner, m. Abigail Gilman, at Boston, Dec. 20, 1705.

ALI (?) DUDLEY died at Brentwood, N. H., May 13, 1763.

ALICE DUDLEY died at B., Oct. 1754.

STEPHEN DUDLEY, of Alton, N. H., m. Elizabeth Deblois, at Boston, June 8, 1823.

MARY DUDLEY, wife of Sir Henry Sidney, died Aug. 1586.

JOANNA DE SUTTON, dau. and heiress of John De Sutton, m. John De Mountford, 1352.

GOV. JOSEPH DUDLEY m. Rebecca Tyng, in 1668.

CAPT. JOHN DUDLEY, (12) son of Samuel D., (5) m. Elizabeth Hilton, dau. of Col. Edward H., of New Market, N. H.

ANNA DUDLEY, dau. of Capt. John D., (12) was born Nov., 1740, and m. John Thing, March, 1760.

REBECCA LYFORD, wife of Hon. Samuel Dudley, was a dau. of Capt. Biley Lyford.

MARY DUDLEY, dau. of Samuel, (18) m. John Haynes.

MEHITABLE, dau. of   do., m. Daniel Stephens.

SUSANNA DUDLEY m. Col. Theophilus Lovering, Jan. 1786, and d. Sept. 3, 1835, at Raymond, N. H.

SAMUEL S. GILMAN was of Kingston, N. H., REUBEN BEAN, of Candia, NATHL. WELLS, of Gilmanton, and Capt. WILLIAM MORRILL, of Brentwood.

MARY DUDLEY, dau. of Daniel, (40) born March 6, 1776.

SUSANNA, dau. of Daniel, (40) b. Sept. 3, 1782, and MEHITABLE, their sister, b. March 29, 1793.

JOHN S. DUDLEY, (59) m. Catharine, dau. of Judge Ebenezer Smith, of Meredith, N. H.

CYRUS DUDLEY, son of TIMO, (61) has a dau. ARABELLA, who m. John Dunbar, of Milwaukie, Wisconsin.

TRUEWORTHY DUDLEY, (25) m. Patty, dau. of his uncle John Gilman.

BETSEY DUDLEY, dau. of Nicholas, (8) m. Benjamin Hill, of Northwood, N. H.

AUTHORS BY THE NAME OF DUDLEY,

WITH THE

TITLES OF THEIR WORKS.

SIR GAMALIEL DUDLEY, *Letter to Prince Rupert*, concerning Sir
Marm. Langdale's march northward, and the victory gained over
him by Fairfax, near Pontefrac. Oxon. 1644, 4to.

JOHN DUDLEY, A. M., Archdeacon of Bedford, *Sermon on Phil. III.
16.* 1729. 8vo. *Two Sermons on the Privileges of the Clergy.*
1731. 8vo.

REV. JOHN DUDLEY, A. M., *Sermon.* Lon. 1807, 4to. 1*s.* 6*d.* *Meta-
morphosis of Sona, a Hindoo Tale.* London, 1811. 8vo.

JOSHUA DUDLEY, *Memoirs of his Life,* written by himself. London,
1772. 8vo.

SIR MATTHEW DUDLEY, *On Insects in the Bark of Decaying Elms and
Ashes.* Phil. Trans. 1705. Abr. V. p. 193.

PAUL DUDLEY, ESQ., F. R. S., *On the Method of Making Sugar from
the Juice of the Maple Tree in New England.* Phil. Trans. 1720.
Abr. VI. 458. *Account of the Poison Wood Tree, (Rhus. Vernix,
Lin.) in New England.* Ib. 507. *On the Method of Discovering
Bee Hives, and obtaining their Honey in New England.* Ib. 509.
Account of the Moose Deer (Cervus Alces, Lin.) in America. Ib.
515. *Account of the Falls of the River Niagara.* Ib. 574. *Ac-
count of the Rattlesnake.* Ib. 642. *An Extraordinary Case by*

Sweating in Hot Roofs of Indian Hot Houses. Ib. 1724. Abr. VII. p. 37. *On some of the Plants in New England, and on remarkable instances of the Nature and Power of Vegetation.* Ib. 57. *Essay on the Natural History of Whales, and on the Ambergris found in Spermaceti Whales.* Ib. 78. *Of a Stone taken out of a Horse.* Ib. 187. *Account of the several Earthquakes which have happened in New England.* Ib. 1735. Abr. VII. 22.

ROBERT DUDLEY, BARON OF DENBIGH AND EARL OF LEICESTER, *Speeches.* Many of these are preserved in the Cabala, Strype's Annals and Peck's Desiderata Curiosa. *Laws and Ordinances set downe by Robt., Earl of Leicester, Captaine Gen. of Her Majesties Forces in the Lowe Countries.* Lon. 4to.

SIR ROBERT DUDLEY, *Account of a Voyage to the Isle of Trinidad,* V. Hackluyt's Voyages, p. 574, 1598. *Catholicon. A Proposition for His Majesty's Service to Bridle the Impertinence of Parliaments. Del l'Arcano del Mere tomo primo diviso nel libro primo e secundo. Tirenze. Tr. Onosri,* 1646.

ANNE DUDLEY, (MRS. SIMON BRADSTREET,) The Tenth Muse lately sprung up in America. By a Gentleman in those parts, &c., printed at London for Stephen Bowtell, 1650, small 8vo.[*]

HON. THOMAS DUDLEY, *Letter to the Countess of Lincoln. Young's Chronicles of the First Planters of Massachusetts Bay,* p. 303.

---

[*] Bibliotheca Britannica.

ELEGIES AND EPITAPHS.

To the Memory of my dear and ever honored father,

THOMAS DUDLEY, ESQ.,

Who deceased July 31, 1653, *and of his age* 77.

By duty bound, and not by custom led
To celebrate the praises of the dead,
My mournful mind, sore pressed, in trembling verse,
Presents my lamentations at his hearse,
Who was my father, guide, instructor, too,
To whom I ought, whatever I could do ;
Nor is 't relation dear, my hand shall tie,
For who more cause to boast his worth, than I ?
Who heard or saw, observed or knew, him better ?
Or who alive, than I, a greater debtor ?
Let malice bite, and envy gnaw its fill—
He was my father, and I 'll praise him, still.
Nor was his name or life led so obscure,
That pity might some trumpeters procure,
Who, after death, might make him falsely seem,
Such, as in life, no man could justly deem.
Well known and loved, where'er he lived, by most,
Both in his native and in foreign coast ;
These, to the world, his merits could make known—
So needs no testimonial from his own :
But now, or never, I must pay my sum ;—
While others tell his worth I 'll not be dumb.
One of the founders, him New England know,
Who stayed thy feeble sides when thou wast low,
Who spent his state, his strength and years, with care,
That after-comers, in them, might have share.
True patriot of this little commonweal,
Who is 't can tax thee aught, but for thy zeal ?
Truth's friend thou wert, to errors still a foe,
Which caused apostates to malign thee so ;

Thy love to true religion e'er shall shine—
My father's God, be God of me and mine;
Upon the earth, he did not build his nest,
But, *as a pilgrim*, what he had, possessed.
High thoughts he gave no harbor in his heart,
Nor honors puffed him up, when he had part;
Those titles loathed, which some too much do love,
For truly his ambition lay *above*;
His humble mind so loved humility,
He left it to his race for legacy;
And oft and oft, with speeches mild and wise,
Gave his in charge, that jewel rich to prize;
No ostentation seen in all his ways,
As in the *mean ones* of our foolish days,
Which all they have, and more, still set to view—
Their greatness may be judged by what they shew;
His thoughts were more sublime, his actions wise—
Such vanities he justly did despise;
Nor wonder, 't was, low things ne'er much did move,
For he a mansion had, prepared above,
For which he sighed, and prayed, and longed, full sore,
He might be clothed upon, forevermore;
Oft spoke of death, and, with a smiling cheer,
He did exult his end was drawing near;
Now fully ripe, as shock of wheat, that's grown,
Death, as a sickle, hath him timely mown,
And, in celestial barn, hath housed him high,
Where storms, or showers, nor aught can damnify;
His generation served, his labors cease,
And to his fathers gathered in peace.
O, happy soul, 'mongst saints and angels blest,
Who, after all his toil, is now at rest;
His hoary head, in righteousness, was found;
As joy in heaven or earth, let praise resound.
Forgotten never be his memory;
His blessing rest on his posterity;
His pious footsteps followed by his race,
At last will bring us to that happy place,
Where we, with joy, each other's face shall see,
And parted more, by death, shall never be.

HIS EPITAPH.

Within this tomb a patriot lies,
That was both pious, just and wise;
To truth, a shield, to right, a wall,
To sectaries a whip and maul;

A magazine of history,
A prizer of good company;
In manners, pleasant and severe,
The good him loved, the bad did fear,
And when his time with years was spent,
If some rejoiced, more did lament.

ANNE BRADSTREET.

AN EPITAPH

*On my dear and ever honored mother, Mrs. Dorothy Dudley, who deceased Decem.
27, 1643, and of her age, 61.*

HERE LYES,
A worthy matron of unspotted life,
A loving mother and obedient wife,
A friendly neighbor, pitiful to poor,
Whom oft she fed and clothéd, with her store;
To servants wisely awful, but yet kind,
And as they did, so they reward did find;
A true instructor of her family,
The which she ordered with dexterity;
The public meetings ever did frequent,
And in her closet constant hours she spent;
Religious in all her words and ways,
Preparing still for death, till end of days;
Of all her children, children lived to see,
Then, dying, left a blessed memòry.

ANNE BRADSTREET.

[At Exeter, N. H.]

Here lyes burried the body of Mr. James Dudley, who departed this life Nove^{mbr} the 14th 1720, in the 57th year of his age.

He was son to the Rev^{nd} Mr. Samuel Dudley, minister of the Gospel at Exeter, and grandson to the Honor. Thomas Dudley, Esqr one of the first governours of New England.

Here lyes ye body of Samuel Dudley, Junr Aged 32 years & about 2 M^{o} Dec^{d} Feb^{ry} ye 16th 1717—18.

Here lyes ye body of Samuel Dudley aged about 5 years Dec^{d} March ye 2^{d} 1717—18.

10

[At Raymond, N. H.]

Hon. John Dudley
died May 21, 1805,
Aet. 80.

This modest stone, what few vain marbles can,
May truly say, " Here lies an honest man."
Calmly he looked on either world, and here
Saw nothing to regret, or there to fear.*

———

Here lyes ye body of Sarah Dudley was born Feb^{ry} ye 25th 1666—7
Departed this life Jan^{ry} ye 24th 1712—13.

———————————————————————

* This was borrowed from Pope's epitaph on Mr. Elijah Fenton.

THE CASTLE OF DUDLEY.

DESCRIPTION.

This old castle stands in the eastern part of the town of Dudley, upon the borders of Staffordshire, Eng., on the summit of a high, rocky hill, whose sides are adorned with beautiful groves. It offers a pleasant and very extensive prospect over several counties and a part of Wales.[*]

The *mansion* once consisted of a variety of buildings, encompassing a court, which was surrounded by an exterior wall, flanked with towers.

The *keep*, or dungeon, which stands in the south-west angle, exhibits evident indications of great antiquity.

Most of the other buildings do not appear more ancient, than the time of Henry VIII. or Elizabeth.

In the kitchen, on the eastern side, are two huge chimneys, the fire-place of one being four and a half yards in width.

A considerable area of land is included within the walls. In the year 1774, this enclosure was leased to a butcher, for thirty pounds per annum.

The spacious hall of the castle formerly contained an oak table seventeen yards in length and one in breadth, constructed of one entire plank, which originally measured twenty-five yards, but being too long for the hall, the superfluous part was cut off, and fashioned into a table for the hall of a neighboring gentleman. The tree from which it was taken is said to have contained more than a hundred tons of timber.[†]

HISTORY.

So much of this castle as time and the destroying hand of man have spared, may claim the honor of being part of one of the oldest fortresses in the English isle.[‡]

---

[*] Plot's Natural History of Staffordshire, ch. x. § 27. Biographia Britannica.
[†] Grose's Antiquities of England and Wales—Staffordshire.
[‡] Camden's Britain in Staffordshire.

Dudo, an Anglo-Saxon, is said to have built and bestowed his name upon it, A. D. 700.*

From the name of this founder of the castle, is derived the present appellation of Dudley, whose orthography has been much varied by writers at different periods.†

At the time of the Norman conquest, as appears from Doomsday Book, this castle was granted to a Norman Baron, by the name of William Fitz Ausculph, who possessed, besides, twenty-five manors in the same county; but it remained not long in the possession of his family, for the daughter of William Fitz Ausculph, marrying Fulk Paganel, brought with her the inheritance of Dudley castle, which descended to her son, Ralph Paganel, who took up arms for the Empress Maud, and fortified it for her, when she contended with King Stephen for the crown of England.

In the reign of Henry II. upon the assessment for the marriage of the king's daughter, Paganel appointed his knights' fees *de veteri feoffmento*, to be fifty in number, and *de novo*, six and a third part.

Afterwards, because he took part with Prince Henry, in an insurrection against his father, the king dismantled his castle of Dudley.‡

Gervase, the son of Ralph Paganel, married Isabel, daughter of Robert, Earl of Leicester, and they had a daughter Hawyse, who married, first, John de Somerie, and secondly, Roger de Berkley, of Berkley Castle.§

Ralph de Somerie, a son of Hawyse and her first husband, John de Somerie, was Baron of Dudley in right of his mother, during the reign of Richard I. In the 17th year of Henry III. A. D. 1233, when it is styled an " honor," it was seized by the king, because its owner, Roger de Somerie, either neglected or refused to appear, when summoned to receive the honor of knighthood.

The writ is preserved, and may be translated thus,—" Because Roger de Somerie, at the feast of Pentecost last past, has not appeared before the king to be girded with the military girdle, the Sheriff of Worcestershire is hereby commanded to seize on the *honor* of Dudley, and all the other lands of the said Roger within his jurisdiction, with all the cattle found upon them, so that nothing may be moved off without the king's permission. Witness the king at Wenlock," &c.¶

---

* Dugdale's Monasticon, Vol. II. p. 122.

† Dugdale, Collins, Kippis, Hayward.

‡ Grose's Antiq. of England and Wales,—Staff.

§ Dugdale's Monasticon, Vol. II. p. 912.

¶ Madox's History of the Exchequer.

In the 48th year of this reign, A. D. 1264, Somerie obtained the royal license to castellate his mansion at Dudley, which had probably remained unfortified ever since its dismantling.

This castle and estate continued in the possession of the Someries till the 15th year of Edward II. A. D. 1322, when John de Somerie, the last male heir of the name, dying, left his two sisters, Margaret and Joan, coheiresses, the elder of whom, Margaret, married Sir John Sutton, of the ancient and respectable Saxon family of Suttons in Nottinghamshire, who became, in her right, Baron of Dudley.*

This nobleman assisting Thomas, Earl of Lancaster, against the ministers of Edward II. was for this cause compelled, in order to save his life, to convey all his right and title in the castle and manor of Dudley, with many other large estates, to Hugh le Despenser, son of Hugh, Earl of Winchester; but in the first year of Edward III. A. D. 1325, he obtained restitution of them all.

One of the Suttons, on account of his owning Dudley castle, was summoned to Parliament in the reign of Henry VI. It continued in their possession till unwillingly conveyed by John Sutton, lord Dudley, to his kinsman the grasping and ambitious John Dudley, Duke of Northumberland. This nobleman, while in its possession, made great repairs, and added a magnificent structure worthy of his wealth and fame, which was called the "New Building." He adorned all parts of the castle with the arms of the noble families, from which, *by his mother*, he was descended, so that, in succeeding times, it might not be supposed an acquisition, but the patrimony of his family.†

This was certainly not very generous, but he went still farther; for, having despoiled his cousin of his castle and estates, he thrust the titles of Dudley and Somerie among his other Baronies, leaving his unhappy kinsman the ridiculous title of lord "Quondam" in their stead.

At length, however, by a sudden revolution of fortune, this lord Quondam again became master of Dudley castle, and his son, Edward, obtained, out of the forfeiture of that potent duke, an ample fortune free from all encumbrances, and a clear title.‡

These estates, Ann, the heiress of Edward Sutton's grandson, Sir Ferdinando, carried in marriage to Humble Ward, Esq., a wealthy goldsmith and jeweller to the Queen of Charles I. Mr. Ward was

* Milles, Brook, Vincent, Dugdale.
† Biographia Britannica.
‡ Dugdale's Baronage.

created Baron, March 23, 1643, by the title of lord Ward, of Birming-
ham, in Warwickshire.

During the civil wars this castle was a royal garrison. In the year
1644, it stood a siege of three weeks, and was relieved, June 11, by a
detachment of the king's forces from Worcester; but May 13, 1646,
it was surrendered to Sir William Brereton by Col. Levison, governor
for the king.

The part taken by lord Ward in these matters, rendered him liable
to some inconveniences from the victorious party; for he was afterwards obliged to ask lenity of the lord Protector, Cromwell, whose privy
council declared in a paper dated July 16, 1656, that they " conceived
the said Mr. Ward an object of his highness' grace and favor."*

The lords Ward seem to have resided here but a short time afterwards, probably on account of its ruinous condition, which was owing
to the injuries received in the siege.

Tradition relates, that, some years since, it served as a retreat to a
band of coiners, who set fire to the buildings—whether accidentally or
purposely, is unknown.

The last information obtained respecting this castle is, that it belonged to the lord Ward, whose predecessor was created Viscount
Dudley and Ward, of Dudley, by George III. April 21, 1763.†

---

* Mr. Astle's Collections.
† Grose's Antiquities of England and Wales.—Staff.

PART SECOND.

THE POSTERITY OF GOV. THOMAS DUDLEY,

THROUGH HIS SON,

GOV. JOSEPH DUDLEY, OF ROXBURY, MASS.

It will be observed, that the descendants of Gov. Joseph Dudley are much less numerous and scattered, than those of Rev. Samuel, of Exeter. Perhaps some of Gov. Joseph's children settled in England, and there died, for I have been unable to find any account of two or three of them in this country, excepting records of their birth.

Rev. Samuel Dudley was forty-one years older than Gov. Joseph, and hence his posterity are now, and ever have been, about one generation in advance of the descendants of the younger brother.

Second Generation in America.

CHILDREN OF GOV. JOSEPH, Son of Gov. Thomas, *Son of Capt. Roger.*

Thomas, b. Feb. 26, 1670 ;

Edward, b. Sept. 4, 1671, d. Feb. 1, 1683, at Roxbury, Mass. ;

Joseph, b. Nov. 8, 1673 ;

‡Judge Paul,* b. Sept. 3, 1675, m. Lucy Wainwright, dau. of Col. John W., of Ipswich, Sept. 15, 1703, d. Jan. 25, 1751, at Roxbury ;

Samuel, b. Sept. 7, 1677 ;

John, b. Feb. 8 or 28, 1679 ;

Rebecca, b. May 16, 1681, m. Samuel Sewall, Jr., Esq., Sept. 15, 1702, who d. Feb. 27, 1751, at Brookline, Mass. Mrs. Rebecca d. April 14, 1761 ;

Catharine, b. Jan. 7, 1683, d. Jan. 7, 1683 ;

---

* Judge Paul had two or three children that died in infancy.

ANN, b. Aug. 27, 1684, m. 1st, John Winthrop, son of Hon. Wait
Still W., Dec. 16, 1707 ; 2d, Mr. Miller, and d. 1776, at New London, Conn. ;

· HON. WILLIAM, b. Oct. 20, 1686, m. Elizabeth Davenport, dau. of
Judge Addington D., March 10, 1721, and d. in 1740 ;

DANIEL, b. Feb. 4, 1689 ;

CATHARINE, 2d., b. Jan. 5, 1690, m. Hon. William Dummer, April
20, 1714, who d. in 1761 ;

MARY, b. Nov. 2, 1692, m. 1st, Francis Wainwright, Jan. 1, 1713 ;
2d, Capt. Joseph Atkins, in 1730.

All of this family, but the last four, are known to have been born at
Roxbury, Mass.

CHILDREN OF PAUL, *Merchant*, SON OF GOV. THOMAS, *Son of Capt. Roger.*

THOMAS, b. March 4, 1677, at Boston, Mass. ;

PAUL, JR., b. Feb. 10, 1681, at Boston.

I know not what became of this family after Paul Dudley's death.

Third Generation in America.

CHILDREN OF HON. WILLIAM, SON OF GOV. JOSEPH, *Son of Gov. Thomas.*

THOMAS, b. Sept. 9, 1731, m. Hannah Whiting, April 26, 1753, who
m. 2dly, Col. Joseph Williams, in 1770, Thomas dying Nov. 9,
1769, at Roxbury ;

JOSEPH, ESQ., b. 1732, m. Lucy ———, d. Sept. 27, 1767, at Boston ;

‡CATHARINE, b.   , m. Peter Johonnot, merchant, who d. at London, Eng., Aug. 8, 1809. Catharine d. June 28, 1769, at Boston ;

ELIZABETH, b. May 16, 1724, m. 1st, Dr. Joseph Richards, March 24,
1749, who d. Feb. 1761, at Dedham ; 2d, Samuel Scarborough,
June 27, 1765, who died July 3, 1789, at Roxbury. Elizabeth d.
Nov. 1, 1805, at Dedham ;

LUCY, b. Feb. 15, 1728, m. Dr. Simon Tufts, Feb. 23, 1749, and d.
Nov. 18, 1768, at Medford ;

‡MARY, b. Aug. 10, 1736, m. John Cotton, and d. Feb. 6, 1796, at
Boston ;

‡REBECCA, b. May 28, 1726, m. 1st, Benjamin Gerrish ; 2d, John Bur-
bige, of Cornwallis, N. S., Oct. 14, 1775, and d. Jan. 30, 1809, at
Concord, N. H. ;

ANN m. John Lovell, and d. April, 1775, at Boston.

Several children of this family were born at Roxbury; the rest at Boston.

Fourth Generation in America.

CHILDREN OF THOMAS, SON OF HON. WILLIAM, *Son of Gov. Joseph.*

WILLIAM, b. Dec. 25, 1753, m. Sarah Williams, Feb. 2, 1774, who d. at Brookline, Sept. 1, 1813; William d. Oct. 4, 1786, at Roxbury;

LIEUT. THOMAS, b. Oct. 27, 1755, m. Abigail Weld, May 14, 1778, and d. at Roxbury;

PAUL, b. July 29, 1757, m. Martha Foster, April 27, 1779, at Roxbury, who was born April 21, 1769, and died Nov. 18, 1821; Paul d. Feb. 22, 1847, at Milford, Me.;

LUCY, b. April 27, 1759, m. Seth T. Whiting, Sept. 11, 1783, and d. about 1846, at Boston;

CATHARINE, b. March 20. 1761, m. Nehemiah Davis, Dec. 27, 1779, at Roxbury, and d. at R.;

REBECCA, b. June 10, 1763, m. Maj. Nathaniel Parker, June 1, 1788, who d. Aug. 11, 1820, aged 60 years; Rebecca d. Sept. 10, 1834, at Brimfield, Mass.;

†JOSEPH G., b. April 29, 1765, d. at Roxbury.

This family were all born at Roxbury.

CHILDREN OF JOSEPH, ESQ., SON OF HON. WILLIAM, *Son of Gov. Joseph.*

JOSEPH; MARY; ANN;—all born at Roxbury.

What became of this family?

Fifth Generation in America.

CHILDREN OF WILLIAM, SON OF THOMAS, *Son of Hon. William.*

SALLY, b. June 19, 1774, m. 1st, John W. Fellows, March 29, 1795; 2d, Thomas Rumrill, and l., 1848, at Roxbury;

BETSEY, b. May 6, 1777, d. Aug. 20, 1778, at R.;

BETSEY, 2d, b. March 25, 1779, m. John Seaver, April 19, 1798, and l., 1848, at R.;

11

Col. Joseph, b. Oct. 16, 1780, m. Pedy Whitney, and d. Feb. 28, 1827, at R. ;

William, b. April 6, 1782, m. Susan Davis, May, 1804, and d. Jan. 15, 1811, at Dudley, Mass. ;

Thomas, b. May 25, 1784, m. Eliza Myland, May, 1805, and d. May, 1831, at Brighton ;

Samuel, b. Aug. 6, 1786, m. Susan D. Brewer, Nov. 18, 1809, and l. 1848, at Brighton.

This family were all born at Roxbury.

CHILDREN OF LIEUT. THOMAS, Son of Thomas, *Son of Hon. William.*

†Hannah, b. April 11, 1781, l., 1848, at Roxbury ;

Thomas, b. March 5, 1783, m. Mary Burrill, and d. Feb. 23, 1826, at R. ;

Twins { Abigail, b. March 11, 1785, d.   ;

{ †Samuel C., b. March 11, 1785, d. at sea ;

David, b. Aug. 23, 1787, m. Hannah Davis, dau. of Moses D., of R., in 1814, and d. at R., April 1, 1841.

They were all born at Roxbury.

CHILDREN OF PAUL, Son of Thomas, *Son of Hon. William.*

†Martha, b. Feb. 9, 1780, at Roxbury, d. Mar. 3, 1805, at Milford, Me. ;

Born at Warwick {

Catharine, b. July 19, 1781, m. Capt. Samuel Bailey, at Milford, Nov. 2, 1802, who was born June 18, 1781, and d. Jan. 18, 1832. Catharine d. March 23, 1821, at Milford ;

Lucy, b. April 15, 1783, m. Col. Ebenezer Webster, Sept. 5, 1805, who was born Oct. 3, 1780, at Bangor. Lucy l. 1848, at Orono, Me. ;

Paul, b. April 11, 1785, m. Mary Freese, Sept. 1, 1808, at Argyle, Me., who was born July 17, 1786, at Bangor. Paul l. 1848, at Milford ;

John, b. March 22, 1787, m. Nancy Cummings, Nov. 29, 1810, who was born Feb. 21, 1790, at Merimack.

Born at Northfield {

Capt. Samuel, b. May 16, 1789, m. Anna Ballard, Jan. 27, 1811, who was born Aug. 10, 1793, at Bucksport, Me. ;

Hannah W., b. Sept. 26, 1794, m. Eli Harthon, Oct. 21, 1811, who was born Jan. 17, 1785, at Brewer, Me. Hannah W. d. Oct. 24, 1811 ;

Arad, b. Oct. 17, 1796, d. Jan. 29, 1818, at Milford, Me.

‡MATILDA, b. Aug. 25, 1800, at Milford, m. Andrew Griffin, of Orono, and d. May 6, 1826.

Sixth Generation in America.

CHILDREN OF COL. JOSEPH, SON OF WILLIAM, *Son of Thomas.*

WILLIAM, b. Oct. 8, 1801, d. Dec. 29, 1801 ;

JOSEPH W., ESQ., b. June 2, 1803, m. Lucy R. Gay, March 11, 1827, and l. 1848, at Roxbury ;

†SARAH W., b. Feb. 20, 1805, l. 1848, at Roxbury ;

ISAAC D., b. Jan. 23, 1807, d. Feb. 7, 1807 ;

†WILLIAM, 2d, b. June 24, 1808, d. Nov. 13, 1833 ;

SAMUEL, b. Dec. 31, 1809, m. Mary E. Gay, Dec. 17, 1837, and l. 1848, at R. ;

PEDY, b. Feb. 7, 1812, m. Lewis Slack, June 2, 1833, and l. 1848, at Boston ;

ELISHA, b. Dec. 9, 1813, d. Oct. 22, 1815 ;

ELISHA, 2d, b. Feb. 2, 1816, d. March 23, 1816 ;

HENRY A. S. D., b. Aug. 13, 1820.

This family were born at Roxbury.

CHILDREN OF WILLIAM, SON OF WILLIAM, *Son of Thomas.*

SUSAN, b. April 12, 1805, bap. May 4, 1806, m. Stephen Sayles, Nov. 10, 1836, l. at Gloucester, R. I. ;

WILLIAM, b. Nov. 10, 1807, bap. Nov. 15, 1807, m. Sophia Miles, June 6, 1847, lives at Blackstone, Mass. ;

†HANNAH, b. March 14, 1809, lives at Blackstone ;

NOAH, b. Dec. 20, 1810, m. 1st, Elizabeth Levenworth, Oct. 15, 1834 ; 2d, Phebe Tourtillot (?) Feb. 23, 1845, lives at Blackstone.

CHILDREN OF THOMAS, SON OF WILLIAM, *Son of Thomas.*

WILLIAM, b. Oct. 12, 1807, at Dudley, Mass.; m. Emily Bemis, of Weston, Feb. 1830, l. 1848, at Weston ;

SAMUEL W., b. Jan. 12, 1810, at Dudley, m. Julia Plimpton, April, 1840, l. 1848, at Boston ;

THOMAS, b. Sept. 2, 1813, m. Mary A. Coffer, April, 1842, lives at West Cambridge ;

†ELIZA, b. March 9, 1815, lives at Boston ;

BENJAMIN, b. June 27, 1818, d. Sept. 5, 1840, at Brighton ;

Caroline F., b. May 18, 1827, m. John W. Mandell, of Brighton, April, 1844, lives at Brookline;

†Sarah R., b. June 4, 1824, lives at Boston.

All of this family, except the first three, were born at Roxbury, Mass.

CHILDREN OF SAMUEL, Son of William, *Son of Thomas.*

Susanna D., b. Jan. 16, 1811, at Roxbury, m. Life Baldwin, 1831, l. at Brighton;

Joseph D., b. April 10, 1812, at R., m. Lovina T. Celley, Jan. 8, 1840, lives at Brighton;

William B., b. June 3, 1816, at Charlton, m. Sarah Richards, in 1841, lives at Brighton;

Samuel W., b. Sept. 29, 1814, at Charlton, m. Sarah B. White, 1838, lives at Brighton;

Rebecca C., b. May 19, 1818, at Needham, lives at Brighton;

Francis W., b. Oct. 20, 1821, at Brighton, lives at B;

Sarah W., b. May 15, 1826, at B., d. Feb. 12, 1837, at B.

CHILDREN OF THOMAS, Son of Lieut. Thomas, *Son of Thomas.*

Mary, b. July 5, 1807, m. Henry H. Williams, of Roxbury;

Elbridge G., b. June 4, 1810, m. Sarah Child, Dec. 3, 1840, lives at Boston;

David, m. Jane Budd, Jan. 16, 1840, lives at Roxbury.

This family were born at Roxbury.

CHILDREN OF DAVID, Son of Lieut. Thomas, *Son of Thomas.*

Rebecca D., b. April 27, 1815, d. Oct. 26, 1815;

Sarah W., b. Nov. 19, 1816, d. Jan. 12, 1817;

Abigail W., b. Oct. 28, 1818, d. young;

Mary A. D., b. Aug. 9, 1821, lives at Roxbury, m. William G. Lewis, Oct. 13, 1841;

Charles D., b. Oct. 2, 1822, d. July 15, 1840;

Abigail W., 2d, b. Nov. 27, 1824, lives at R.;

Julia M., b. Feb. 2, 1827, d. March 16, 1827;

Caroline W., b. July 25, 1830, lives at R.;

Hannah M., b. Sept. 5, 1832, lives at R.;

George F., b. Jan. 14, 1835, lives at R.

This family were all born at Roxbury.

CHILDREN OF PAUL, Son of Paul, *Son of Thomas.*

Arad, b. March 23, 1809, m. Delana L. Pratt, July 3, 1833, at Bangor, who was born April 5, 1815, at Leeds, Me. ;

†Rebecca F., b. May 24, 1811, d. at Milford, Me. ;

Charlotte I., b. Sept. 8, 1813, m. William Howard, Nov. 25, 1841, who was born Nov. 7, 1802, at Bangor ;

†Susan P., b. July 5, 1815, d. at Milford ;

William F., b. June 14, 1818 ;

George F., b. June 20, 1821 ;

Ebenezer W., b. June 6, 1824 ;

Margaret A., b. July 12, 1830.

This family were born at Milford, Me.

CHILDREN OF JOHN, Son of Paul, *Son of Thomas.*

Lucy F., b. Oct. 29, 1811, m. Richard Blaisdell, May 18, 1827, who was born Oct. 29, 1799 ;

Daniel, b. Jan. 14, 1816 ;

Olivia C., b. Oct. 5, 1817, m. William Bailey, March 26, 1838, who was born July 29, 1814 ;

James C., b. Nov. 19, 1823 ;

John A., b. Jan. 18, 1828.

They were born at Milford, Me.

CHILDREN OF CAPT. SAMUEL, Son of Paul, *Son of Thomas.*

William B., b. April 29, 1812, m. Thankful S. Collins, Nov. 1, 1835 ;

John, b. June 29, 1814, m. Hannah Babbage, dau. of Capt. John B., Aug. 26, 1838, at Argyle, Me.   Miss B. was born June 19, 1818, at Deer Isle ;

Mary A., b. Nov. 21, 1816, m. William H. Page ;

Samuel, b. May 9, 1819, m. Susan J. Comstock, July 13, 1845, who was born May 18, 1825, at Argyle, Me. ;

Charles, b. May 21, 1821, d. July 30, 1822 ;

Charles, 2d, b. May 18, 1823 ;

Isaac, b. March 25, 1825, m. Caroline Emerson, Aug. 27, 1845, at Passadumkeag, who was born Dec. 20, 1827 ;

Paul, b. May 18, 1827 ;

Caroline M., b. June 7, 1829 ;

Francis H., b. Oct. 5, 1832.

This family were born, and lived, at Milford, Me.

Seventh Generation in America.

THE DAUGHTER OF JOSEPH W., Esq., Son of Col. Joseph, *Son of William.*

Lucy, b. at Roxbury, m. Ebenezer Rumrill, of Roxbury.

CHILDREN OF SAMUEL, Son of Col. Joseph, *Son of William.*

Mary E., b. Nov. 13, 1838 ; Sarah W., b. April 8, 1840 ; Samuel, Jr., b. April 24, 1841 ; Joseph W., b. June 8, 1843 ;—all born at Roxbury, Mass.

THE SON OF ARAD, Son of Paul, *Son of Paul.*

Alonzo, b. April 30, 1836, at Milford, Me.

CHILDREN OF WILLIAM B., Son of Capt. Samuel, *Son of Paul.*

Melissa A., b. June 2, 1836 ; Mary M., b. Aug. 24, 1837 ; Phebe B., b. Jan. 26, 1840 ; Charles H., b. June 21, 1842, d. May 19, 1844 ; William H., b. June 11, 1846 ;—all born at Milford, Me.

THE DAUGHTER OF JOHN, Son of Capt. Samuel, *Son of Paul.*

Hellen Mar, b. June 29, 1839, at Milford.

CHILDREN OF SAMUEL, Son of Capt. Samuel, *Son of Paul.*

Sarah J., b. April 29, 1846, at Milford ;
Mary A., b. Aug. 3, 1847, at   do.

THE DAUGHTER OF ISAAC, Son of Capt. Samuel, *Son of Paul.*

Clara, b. June 1, 1846, d. Nov. 26, 1846, at Milford.

THE POSTERITY OF FRANCIS DUDLEY,*

THROUGH HIS SONS,

JOSEPH, JOHN AND FRANCIS, JR.

FRANCIS DUDLEY, a supposed relation of Gov. Thomas D., was born in England, and, immigrating to this country, settled at Concord, Mass., perhaps about 1663. He m. Miss Sarah Wheeler of C. Oct. 26, 1665, and probably remained in that town till his decease. Mrs. Sarah Dudley, the wife, died Dec. 12, 1713, at Concord.

First Generation in America.

CHILDREN OF FRANCIS DUDLEY.

MARY m. Joseph Fletcher; JOSEPH m. Abigail Gobble, 1691, and d. Nov. 3, 1702, at Concord; SAMUEL, b. 1666, m. 1st, Abigail King, Nov. 1, 1704; 2d, Lydia   , and d. 17** at Sutton, Mass. The wife d. Aug. 9, 1720; SARAH d. Aug. 4, 1701; JOHN m. Hannah Poultier, of Medford, May 16, 1697. This lady d. Dec. 20, 1707; FRANCIS, JR. m. 1st, Sarah   , 2d, Abigail   .

---

* There is a tradition among the descendants of Francis Dudley of Concord, that he, with his two brothers, immigrated to Massachusetts from Ireland, being non-conformists, and Francis settled at Concord, Mass., William in Connecticut, and the third brother in Rhode Island; and each left posterity.

I very much doubt the correctness of a part of this story, for Francis married at Concord as late as 1665, and, afterwards had a large family of children, which proves that he was a youth at the time of his settling in Concord, about 1663, while William of Guilford, Ct., was of adult age as early as 1637, when he arrived at Boston, from England, and, therefore, could not be supposed a brother to this Francis Dudley.

Second Generation.

CHILDREN OF JOSEPH,* Son of Francis.

Abigail, b. June 11, 1692, m. John Davis, Dec. 17, 1713; Sarah, b. June 11, 1692; James; Jane, b. March 26, 1693; Joseph, Jr. b. April 20, 1697, m. Mary Chandler, Oct. 2, 1718; Benjamin, b. March 20, 1698, d. at Sudbury; Mary, b. Feb. 8, 1700; Sibella, b. Sep. 22, 1702, m. Jonathan Brown, Sep. 5, 1718. This family were all born at Concord, Mass.

CHILDREN OF JOHN, Son of Francis.

John, Jr., b. Aug. 16, 1699, m. Mary   , d. probably, at Acton; Hannah, b. March 9, 1703, d. at Concord, Oct. 18, 1716; Sarah, b. Feb. 16, 1705; *A son*, b. Dec. 20, 1707;—all born at Concord, Mass.

CHILDREN OF FRANCIS, JR.

Samuel, b. at Concord, Aug. 1700; *Others*, doubtless, whose names are unknown to me.

Third Generation.

CHILDREN OF JOSEPH, JR.,§ Grandson of Francis.

Joseph, 3d., b. July 24, 1719, m. Mary Brown, Jan. 16, 1741; Eliza, b. Feb. 14, 1721; Mary, b. Jan. 17, 1723; Samuel, b. March 7, 1725; Lucy, b. Apr. 1, 1727, m. John Perry, Dec. 6, 1744; Abigail, b. about 1730, m. Samuel Howe, April 12, 1750; Ebenezer, b. about 1735, m. Grace   , d. at Sudbury. The wife d. at Hebron, Me., Sept. 25, 1821; William, b. about 1740, m. Judith Curtis; Mary, 2d, b. Oct. 9, 1741;—*all born at Concord, Mass.*; Sarah, b. at Sudbury, Oct. 13, 1754; Nahum, b. at S., May 4, 1757; Daniel, b. at S., Feb. 22, 1763.

---

* There were two or three Josephs in Sudbury, whose children were nearly cotemporary; and the town records not being sufficiently explicit in respect to parentage, some mistakes may possibly be detected in these records of their families. See the record of Joseph, Jr's, family.

§ See the note annexed to the family record of Joseph, 3d.

CHILDREN OF JOHN, Jr., Grandson of Francis.

John, 3d, b. Mar. 13, 1729; Peter, b. Aug. 26, 1731; Daniel, b. June 22, 1733, m. Hannah Farrar, June 28, 1757; James, b. Nov. 21, 1734, m. 1st, Mehitable   ; 2d, Miss Piper, was in the French war; John, 2d, b. Jan. 11, 1737. This family were born at Concord, Mass.

Fourth Generation.

CHILDREN OF WILLIAM, Son of Joseph, Jr.

William, Jr., b. July 25, 1763, m. 1st, Ann Moulton, July 7, 1791; 2d, Unity Rice, who d. 1835; Ephraim, b. Jan. 29, 1766, d. at Castleton, Vt.; Nathaniel was drowned in Johnson Pond; Jason m. Betsey   , d. May 20, 1812. The wife d. June 18, 1812, at Sudbury; Nancy m. Thomas Piper, May 3, 1808; *A son* was killed by the Captain on board a war-ship, aged about 20 years, unmarried; Abigail m. Paul Lowker, and died. They were born at Sudbury, Mass.

CHILDREN OF JOSEPH, 3d, great-grandson of Francis.

Benjamin, b. Nov. 25, 1741, m. Mary   , who died at Sudbury, Jan. 21, 1814; Joseph, 4th, b. Sep. 16, 1743, m. 1st, Sarah   ; 2d, Eunice Derby, of Concord, July 28, 1789; Samuel, b. Sept. 29, 1746, m. 1st, Lucy   ; 2d, Sarah   ; †Mary, b. Aug. 4, 1749, d. Feb. 27, 1819, at Wayland, formerly East Sudbury; Nathan, b. June 17, 1755, m. 1st, Sarah Munroe; 2d, Mrs. Hannah Lane, and d. about 1832, at Lexington; Abishai, b. July 24, 1758; Abigail, b. June 13, 1761, m. Elijah Goodman, June 16, 1777; Rebecca, b. Aug. 28, 1763— all born at Concord, Mass.; Submit,* b. Aug. 14, 1765, at Sudbury; Dr. Moses,* b. Jan. 31, 1769, at S., m. Abigail Robie, Jan. 16, 1798, and d. at Westmoreland, N. H.; Luther, b. May 5, 1772 at S., m. Martha Wellington, Nov. 20, 1791.

CHILDREN OF CAPT. EBENEZER, Son of Joseph, Jr.

Abigail, b. June 3, 1758, m. Jonathan Walker, d. at Petersham; Nathan, b. Mar. 20, 1760, m. Jane Dudley, Mar. 14, 1779; Rachel,

---

* The Sudbury town records read thus :—"Submit, Moses, &c., sons of Joseph and Mary Dudley." But *which* Joseph and Mary? for there were two cotemporary.

12

b. Feb. 23, 1761, m. John Roberts, d. at S.; David, b. Oct. 1, 1763 m. 1st, Rebecca Buckman, of Worcester, Mass., Sept. 11, 1791 ; 2d, Charity Tuel, Nov. 25, 1802; Eunice m. Nicholas Manson, d. at Boston; Susan m. Erasmus Babbitt; Ebenezer, Jr., b. April 20, 1771, m. Abigail Murdock, dau. of Ephraim M., Dec. 10, 1798, d. Aug. 2, 1831, at West Roxbury. They were all born at Sudbury.

CHILDREN OF DANIEL, Son of John, Jr.

Daniel, b. March 27, 1758, at Concord, m. Lucy Vose, of C., July 23, 1787; Josiah, b. at C., m. Abigail Brown, of Sudbury, Aug. 31, 1797.

CHILDREN OF JAMES, Son of John, Jr.
By the first wife.

James, b. March 31, 1757, at Concord, m. Mary Raymond of Acton, April 21, 1763; Lucy, b. March 17, 1759, at C.
By the second wife.

Samuel lives at Mount Holly, Vermont; *A daughter;* Paul, b. Mar. 7, 1771, at Acton, m. 1st, Abi Durant, who d. at Concord, 1839; 2d, Hannah Nichols, of Westford, who is living. He died June 8, 1843, at Acton.

Fifth Generation.

CHILDREN OF BENJAMIN, Son of Joseph, 3d.

Abijah, bap. Aug. 25, 1799, m. Susan   , d. at S., April 24, 1840 ; Silvia, bap. Aug. 25, 1799 ; Phebe, bap. Aug. 25, 1799 ; Benjamin, Jr., bap. Nov. 3, 1799 ; Lorunama, bap. Nov. 18, 1804; Samuel S., bap. Aug. 31, 1806 ;. Sibbel, bap. April 9, 1808 ; Moses, bap. June 7, 1811 ; Timothy, bap. July 3, 1814, d. Aug. 15, 1817, at S. They were all baptized at Sudbury.

CHILDREN OF JOSEPH, 4th, Son of Joseph, 3d.

Timothy, b. Dec. 3, 1768; Sarah, b. July 25, 1772 ; Molly, b. Nov. 7, 1774; Joseph, 5th, b. Sep. 2, 1787 ; Eunice, b. Dec. 18, 1778—all born at Concord, Mass.

CHILDREN OF SAMUEL, Son of Joseph, 3d.

Lucy, b. June 3, 1774; Polly, b. Nov. 27, 1776, d. at Concord; Polly, 2d, b. May 25, 1778; Betsey, b. April 2, [1781; Rebecca, b. Sept. 23, 1784; Sally, b. Oct. 28, 1787;—all born at Concord, Mass.

CHILDREN OF NATHAN, Son of Joseph, 3d.

Sarah m. John Viles, of Lexington; John, b. Nov. 18, 1789, m. Esther E. Smith, lives at Boston; Polly m. Thomas Johnson, of Woburn; Betsey m. Solomon Harrington, lives at Boston; Rebecca m. William Shaw, of Woburn, lives at Lexington. They were all born at Lexington, Mass.

CHILDREN OF LUTHER, Son of Joseph, 3d.

Mary, b. March 3, 1797; Warren, b. July 4, 1800; Moses, b. Oct. 11, 1794;—all born at Wayland, formerly called East Sudbury.

CHILDREN OF DANIEL, Jr., Grandson of Joseph, 3d.

Lewis, b. June 8, 1799, m. Margaret Winch, Jan. 7, 1819; and was drowned in Johnson Pond, Jan. 16, 1838. Thomas H., b. March 27, 1788, d. May 8, 1833, at W.; Joseph, b. Sep. 24, 1789; John V. m. Eliza Harrington, July 18, 1819, d. Oct. 17, 1837, at Wayland. This family were born at Wayland, Mass.

CHILDREN OF WILLIAM, Jr., Grandson of Joseph, Jr.

John M., b. Oct. 24, 1791, m. Elizabeth Brown, of Scarboro', Me., and d. at S.; Clarissa, b. Sep. 9, 1798, m. Thomas R. Hanson, and d. at Weymouth, June, 1847; Samuel, b. April 18, 1793, m. Nancy Brown, who d. at Portland. Col. Samuel was murdered at New York; William R., b. March 6, 1807, m. Mary   , ; †Sarah A., b. May 25, 1810, d. at W., March 24, 1844; Benjamin A., b. Sep. 6, 1811, m. Rosalie Heard, May 8, 1839; Nathaniel C., b. Jan. 17, 1813, m. Philindia   , who d. April 16, 1838, at Wayland. They were all born at Wayland, Mass.

CHILDREN OF JASON, Son of William, *Son of Joseph,* (2)

Betsey, b. at Sudbury, d. Feb. 13, 1813, at S.; *Others,* probably, b. at S.

CHILDREN OF DAVID, Son of Capt. Ebenezer, *Son of Joseph, Jr.*

Daniel, b. Oct. 9, 1792, at Sudbury, m. 1st, Lovisa Dudley, Nov. 28, 1816; 2d, Jane Churchill, June 9, 1835. Mrs. Lovisa was born 1794, d. 1835, in Maine; Rebecca, b. March 9, 1794, at Paris, Me., m. Eli Washburn, Feb. 1, 1815; David, b. Sept. 9, 1796, at Paris; Betsey, b. Feb. 13, 1798, at P., m. Aaron Davis, Nov. 15, 1844; Clarissa, b. April 13, 1800, at P., m. Galen Soule, June 7, 1826; Perrin, b. Feb. 3, 1803, at P., m. Paulina Felt, April 6, 1826; Lodicia, b. Nov. 8, 1805, at P., m. Seth Perkins, March 5, 1829; Arvilla, b. Dec. 7, 1807, m. Eli Bryant, Nov. 30, 1830; Ann, b. June 19, 1809, m. John Day, Nov. 25, 1845; Alfred, b. Jan. 9, 1811; Charlotte, b. June 1, 1813, m. Jonathan Day, May 15, 1832; Sidney, b. Feb. 9, 1817; Gilbert, b. Sept. 10, 1818, m. Mahala Curtis, March 5, 1844; Ansel, b. Feb. 9, 1821; Josiah A., b. March 11, 1823, in Maine.

CHILDREN OF EBENEZER, Jr., Grandson of Joseph, Jr.

Abigail H., b. Dec. 21, 1800, m. John Brown, of Billerica; Ebenezer, 3d, b. Jan. 25, 1802, m. Elizabeth Richards, dau. of Lemuel R.; Charity M., b. Jan. 20, 1804, m. 1st, John A. Davis; 2d, Samuel Briggs, of Dorchester; William D., b. Feb. 1, 1806, m Elizabeth Lufkin; Ephraim M., b. May 23, 1808, m. Elmira Swallow, dau. of John S.; Sarah M., b. Feb. 3, 1810, m. Mottram V. Arnold, of Brighton; †Ann Maria, b. March 1, 1812; †Betsey S., b. May 25, 1814, d. at West Roxbury, Jan. 26, 1837; Charlotte, b. March 26, 1817, m. Alexander Mair, of Boston; †Henry, b. Jan. 13, 1821. This family were all born at West Roxbury, Mass.

CHILDREN OF JOSIAH, Son of Daniel, *Son of John, Jr.*

Elizabeth, b. March 25, 1798; Josiah, Jr., b. Nov. 9, 1799, died; Josiah, 2d, b. Oct. 9, 1800; Rebecca, b. Oct. 9, 1801, d. April 7, 1801; Abigail, b. Oct. 2, 1803; Joseph, b. Sept. 25, 1812;—all born at Wayland.

THE SON OF SAMUEL, Son of James, *Son of John, Jr.*

Samuel R., Esq., of Pleasant Valley, Fulton Co., N. Y.; Asa W., of Mount Holly, Vt.

CHILDREN OF PAUL, Son of James, *Son of John, Jr.*

James, b. Sept. 20, 1797, at Acton, m. Mary A. Proctor, of Litteton, d. Sept. 1831, at Richmond Co., Virginia ; Paul, Jr.,* b. Sept. 19, 1799, at Acton, m. Rebecca Adams, of Concord, who was b. Aug. 30, 1796, lives at C.; Mary, b. May 28, 1802, m. Rodolpho Parker, of Chelmsford ; John L., b. Oct. 26, 1805, m. Rebecca Brown, of Andover, d. Nov. 1841 ; Josiah P., b. May 22, 1808, m. 1st, Deborah Bosworth ; 2d, Aroline Fry, of Lowell ; Asa P., b. Nov. 13, 1811, m. Almira Bright, Nov. 3, 1839, lives at Acton.

Sixth Generation.

CHILDREN OF CAPT. ABIJAH, Son of Benjamin.

Sarah, d. April 24, 1840, at Sudbury, Mass. ; Emily L., b. Nov. 8, 1818, m. Jonas D. Morse, of Marlboro', Oct. 18, 1838 ; Amos A., b. June 17, 1821, d. April 11, 1822 ; Amos A., 2d, b. March 23, 1823 ; Lyman G., b. April 3, 1825 ; Samuel E., b. July 8, 1827 ; George G., b. May 7, 1830, d. Oct. 1, 1832. This family were born at Sudbury, Mass.

CHILDREN OF BENJAMIN, Jr., Grandson of Joseph, 3d.

Josiah, b. at Wayland, Mass.; and probably *others* whose names are unknown to me.

CHILDREN OF JOHN, Son of Nathan, *Son of Joseph, 3d.*

John W., b. and d. at Lexington, Mass. ; Eliza, b. at L., m. George W. Fowle ; Sarah D., b. at M., m. Rev. Joseph B. Holman ; Martha A., b. at L., lives at Boston ; Maj. Nathan A. M., b. at L., Aug. 20, 1825, m. Elizabeth G. Jewett, of Roxbury ; Caroline M., lives at Boston ; Andrew J., d. young, 1828 ; Charles H., lives at Boston ; John E., lives at B.

CHILDREN OF JOHN V., Son of Daniel, Jr.

Moses, b. Jan. 3, 1820, at Wayland ; James W., b. March 27, 1824, at Wayland.

---

* Paul, Jr., has one son, at least, whose name is unknown to me.

CHILDREN OF COL. SAMUEL, Son of William, Jr.

Ann E. m. J. Warren Thayer, lives at Beloit, Wisconsin.

CHILDREN OF BENJAMIN, Son of William, Jr.

Rosalia A., b. at Wayland; Edward M., b. at W.

CHILDREN OF NATHANIEL C., Son of William, Jr.

Anna M.; Caroline E.; One d. May 7, 1838, at W.

CHILDREN OF DEA. DANIEL, Son of David, *Son of Capt. Ebenezer.*

Livy, b. Jan. 29, 1818, m. Sarah Brown; Josiah, b. July 12, 1820; Cyrus B., b. Aug. 2, 1812, d. Nov. 27, 1845; Louisa, b. Nov. 4, 1825; Ann, b. April 14, 1827; Rebecca, b. Oct. 21, 1829; Laura, b. April 6, 1837; Augusta, b. Jan. 24, 1839; Samuel H., b. May 31, 1842; Jabez, b. Nov. 2, 1844; Oliver P., b. May 4, 1847. This family reside in the State of Maine.

CHILDREN OF JAMES, Son of Paul, *Son of John, Jr.*

Mary A., b. 1825, d. Sept. 1839, at Concord; James H., b. 1827, lives at Boston; Leonard, b. 1829, d. at sea, 1831; Maria E., b. April 28, 1832, at Lexington, Mass., lives at Boston; Paul A., b. Feb. 8, 1842.

CHILDREN OF JOHN L., Son of Paul, *Son of James, Son of John, Jr.*

Marcus L., b. at Dighton; Eliza, b. at Baltimore, Md., d. at B.; Maria, b. and lives at B.; Rebecca B., b. and lives at B.; Jane C., b. and lives at B.; John, b. 1839, d. 1840, at B.; Therxina, b. and d. at B.

CHILDREN OF JOSIAH P., Son of Paul, *Son of James, Son of John, Jr.*

By the first wife.

Deborah B., b. 1841.

By the second Wife.

Aroline, b. and d. at Lowell; *Another*, b. Feb. 1848, at L.

THE SON OF ASA P., Son of Paul, *Son of James, Son of John, Jr.*
Charles G. B., b. May 23, 1843, at Acton.

[I know not, to which of the foregoing families, the following persons belong.]

Dr. Moses, bro. of Jonas. Jonas, d. at Wayland, Oct. 5, 1836. Sally m. Artemas Greenwood, of Needham, Oct. 19, 1823. Amanda, of Wayland, m. John Proctor, of Natick, March 29, 1836. Joseph M., of Wayland, m. Ann Pratt, Jan. 2, 1837. Lucy J. m. Elbridge J. Carter, of Natick, May 23, 1839. Olive A., of Framingham, m. Samuel Davis, Feb. 25, 1841. Elizabeth, of Wayland, m. David Spofford of Weston, April 1, 1841. Daniel, son of Joseph, d. April 24, 1808. Wm. d. May 31, 1825, at E. Sudbury. James, of Concord, m. Mary Raymond, of Acton, April 21, 1763. Joseph, son of Joseph, and Mary his wife, b. at Sudbury, March 20, 1760. Joseph, of Acton, m. Lucy Maynard, of Sudbury, June 16, 1791. Josiah, of Acton, m. Betsey Smith, of Sudbury, July 6, 1792. Elizabeth, of Wayland, m. Sherebiah Evans, of Milton, Jan. 29, 1795. Sally, of Wayland, m. Artemas Greenwood, of Needham, Oct. 19, 1823. Jonas, d. Oct. 5, 1836, at Wayland. Mary, dau. of Joseph and Mary his wife, b. at Sudbury, June 17, 1752, m. Joseph Nichols, Oct. 25, 1775.

CHILDREN OF CALEB DUDLEY, *who died at Petersham, Mass.*

Caleb, Jr.; John; Mary Ann m. Mr. Burnett, and lives at South Orange, Mass.; Nathan, m. Miss Hatstat, dau. of Thomas Hatstat.

CHILDREN OF NATHAN, Son of Caleb.

Thomas and Lincoln, of Boston; Elvira; Frances, of Petersham; Ezra, b. May 28, 1829, at New Salem, Mass.; Charles, b. April 1, 1831, and Horace, b. at N. S. The first four were born at Petersham, Mass.

THE POSTERITY OF FRANCIS DUDLEY,

THROUGH HIS SON,

SAMUEL, ESQ., OF SUTTON.

Second Generation in America.

CHILDREN OF SAMUEL, Esq., Son of Francis.

SAMUEL, JR., b. July 28, 1705, m. Miss Abigail Waters, and d. about 1750, at Littleton, being killed by the accidental discharge of a gun; FRANCIS, b.   , Dec. 10, 1706, m. Sibella   ; DAVID,* b. Nov. 4, 1709, m. Hannah   ; JONATHAN,* b. Nov. 4, 1709, m. Hannah Putnam, Aug. 18, 1736, at Sutton; this lady d. May 21, 1801, at Sutton; ABIGAIL,* b. Nov. 4, 1709; SARAH, b. July 28, 1713;—all born at Concord, Mass.; ABIGAIL, 2d, b. Oct. 28, 1714; MARY, b. Feb. 22, 1716; PATTY, b. Sept. 13, 1718; ROGERS, b. Aug. 9, 1720, m. Mary Sibley, May 31, 1743, at Sutton; PAUL, b. Sept. 24, 1721; CHARLES, b. Dec. 10, 1722; WILLIAM, b. May 28, 1726;—the last seven born at Littleton.

Third Generation.

CHILDREN OF SAMUEL, JR., GRANDSON OF FRANCIS.

SAMUEL, 3d, b. Jan. 14, 1729, m. Rebecca Hayward, of Acton, about 1755, d. at Waterford, Me., 1803; ABIGAIL, b. Sept. 13, 1788; STEPHEN, b. July 2, 1735, m. Lydia Harwood, of Littleton, and died about 1784, in South Carolina; LOUISA, b. June 12, 1737; JOSEPH, b. Aug. 12, 1739, was slain at Quebec, during the French war; ABIGAIL, 2d, b. Oct. 29, 1741; this lady "intended" marrying Timothy Fox, Jan. 22, 1764. They were all born at Littleton, Mass.

---

* These were children of a triple birth.

CHILDREN OF FRANCIS, Son of Samuel, Esq.

Martha, b. June 27, 1736, m. Simon Gleason, June 2, 1764, at Sutton; Mary, b. Dec. 6, 1740, m. Joel Wheeler, Dec. 19, 1765, at S.; Sarah, b. June 7, 1744; Francis, Jr., b. Feb. 18, 1748, m. Elizabeth Whipple, May 21, 1771, at Sutton. They were born at Sutton, Mass.

CHILDREN OF DAVID, Son of Samuel, Esq.

Betty, b. July 26, 1738; Hannah, b. Feb. 14, 1744; Abel, b. Oct. 21, 1746, m. Sarah   , and d. at Sutton, Feb. 13, 1813; Timothy, b. Aug. 16, 1751; Abigail, b. June 15, 1758, m. Isaac Gleason, April 12, 1774, at Sutton; Lucy, b. Aug. 2, 1761, m. John Totman, Nov. 22, 1784, at Sutton. They were all born at Sutton.

CHILDREN OF JONATHAN, Son of Samuel, Esq.

Jonathan, Jr., b. March 22, 1738, m. 1st, Mary Garfield, Feb. 1, 1763; 2d, Jemima Stearns, June 22, 1786; Mrs. Jemima d. at Sutton, 1840; Hannah, b. Jan. 20, 1740; John, b. Aug. 20, 1743, m. Mary Morse, Oct. 13, 1768, at Sutton; Mrs. Mary D. m. 2dly, Solomon Leland, Esq., 1791; Prudence, b. May 4, 1747, m. Henry King, June 18, 1772, at Sutton; Anna, b. April 9, 1753, m. Alpheus Marble, Dec. 15, 1774, at Sutton; Samuel, b. Jan. 4, 1755; Peter, b. Jan. 10, 1758, m. Sarah Chase, Dec. 12, 1781, at Sutton, and d. Sept. 8, 1836, at S.; Mrs. Sarah D. d. at S., Feb. 24, 1836. They were all born at Sutton.

CHILDREN OF ROGERS, Son of Samuel, Esq.

Mary, b. April 20, 1746; David, b. Jan. 14, 1750, m. Lois Whitney, Dec. 16, 1773, at Sutton; Mary, 2d, b Dec. 14, 1751;—all born at Sutton.

Fourth Generation.

CHILDREN OF SAMUEL, 3d, Son of Samuel, Jr.

Rebecca, b. April 27, 1757; Mary, b. Feb. 29, 1760; Samuel, b. March 6, 1762, d. at Harvard, 1834; Joseph, b. July 11, 1765, d. at Waterford, Me., 1837; Josiah, b. Dec. 26, 1767, m. Betsey Smith, of Acton, 1792, l. at Pamelia, N. Y., 1848. They were born at Littleton, Mass.

13

CHILDREN OF STEPHEN, Son of Samuel, Jr.

Stephen, Jr.,* d. at Cato, Cayuga Co., N. Y., Aug. 1826 ; Lydia, b. Aug. 17, 1759, d. Dec. 6, 1759, at Littleton ; Abigail, b. July 3, 1764 ; Joseph, b. Sept. 30, 1766 ; Samuel, b. April 29, 1769 ; Mary, b. Sept. 22, 1771, m. 1st, Mr. Barton, of Andover, Vt. ; 2d, Jesse Heald, of Chester, Vt. ; Gen. Peter, b. Nov. 29, 1773, m.   , d. July, 1847, at Peru, Bennington Co., Vt. ; Hannah, b. July 1, 1775 ; Jonathan, b. Sept. 28, 1778, lives at Pittsfield, Loraine Co., Ohio ; Ebed M. M. ; Asa, b. June 30, 1782. They were all born at Littleton.

CHILDREN OF FRANCIS, Jr., Grandson of Samuel, Esq.

Mary, b. Dec. 19, 1771 ; Francis, 3d, b. Feb. 5, 1774 ; Elizabeth, b. Jan. 5, 1776 ; Samuel, b. April 1, 1781 ; Beulah, b. April 2, 1783 ; Simon, b. April 23, 1787. They were all born at Sutton, Mass.

CHILDREN OF ABEL, Son of David, *Son of Samuel*, Esq.

Hannah, b. Jan. 12, 1769 ; David, b. Jan. 1, 1771, d. at Sutton, Sept. 14, 1826 ; Tabitha, b. Aug. 1, 1774, m. Daniel Torrey, May 26, 1791, at S. ; Abigail, b. Sept. 10, 1776 ; Abel, Jr., b. Sept. 15, 1780, m. Polly Drake, supposed to be a sister of Francis Drake ; she d. Feb. 10, 1817, at Shrewsbury ; Sarah, b. April 15, 1782, m. Dexter Rawson, Feb. 28, 1803, at Sutton, lives at Webster, Mass. They were born at Sutton.

CHILDREN OF JONATHAN, Jr., Grandson of Samuel, Esq.

Jonathan, 3d, b. Feb. 27, 1766, m. Lydia Marble, Nov. 27, 1788, at Sutton, d. at S., Oct. 30, 1845 ; Mrs. Lydia d. at S., Aug., 1827 ; Hannah, b. March 24, 1768, m. Archelaus Sibley, Oct. 11, 1789, at S. ; Samuel, b. April 9, 1771 ; Elijah, b. July 26, 1764, m. Elizabeth Weld, Oct. 30, 1791, d. Sept. 17, 1805, at Roxbury ; Mary, b. March 24, 1773 ; Lucy, b. May 10, 1787, m. Reuben Eaton, Jr., Sept. 15, 1808, at S. ; Jemima, b. about 1789, m. Warren Hathaway, Nov. 27, 1808, at S. ; Sally, b. about 1791 ; Prudence, b. about 1793. They were all born at Sutton, Mass.

---

* Rev. Ira, a son of this gentleman, resides at Baldwinsville, N. Y.

CHILDREN OF JOHN, Son of Jonathan, *Son of Samuel, Esq.*

John, Jr., b. Oct. 19, 1769, m. Deborah Marble, Feb. 28, 1792, at Sutton; Joseph, b. Sept. 18, 1773, m. Abigail Potter, March 25, 1794, at Sutton; Mrs. Abigail, *widow*, d. Jan. 7, 1837, at S.; Sarah, b. Jan. 22, 1779; James, b. Nov. 23, 1783.

CHILDREN OF PETER, Son of Jonathan, Jr.

Caleb, b. Sept. 14, 1782, at Sutton, Mass.; Phebe, b. March 21, 1784, at S., m. David Dudley, Feb. 18, 1804, at S.

CHILDREN OF DAVID, Son of Rogers, *Son of Samuel, Esq.*

John; David, Jr., b. 1781, d. Nov. 3, 1836, at Sutton; Luther; Sally; Betsey, b. Feb. 9, 1787, m. John March, Aug. 18, 1811; Joseph, b. March 14, 1790; Amasa, b. Oct. 17, 1792; Polly;— all born at Sutton.

CHILDREN OF GEN. PETER, Son of Stephen, *Son of Samuel, Jr.*

James M., Esq., of Oppenheim, Fulton Co., N. Y.; *Two other sons and eight daughters.*

Fifth Generation.

CHILDREN OF ABEL, Jr., Grandson of David, *Son of Samuel, Esq.*

Rinda, b. Aug. 19, 1802, m. Nahum Ball, lives at Woonsocket Falls, R. I.; Gerry, b. Oct. 20, 1803, m. Betsey K. Bellows, Nov. 18, 1827, at Shrewsbury, and d. Jan. 25, 1835, at Shrewsbury; †David, b. June 15, 1805, lives at Shrewsbury; †Eliza, b. Aug. 20, 1806, lives at Valley Falls, R. I.; †Abigail, b. June 2, 1808, lives at Valley Falls; Sumner, b. Sept. 4, 1810, m.; Rufus H., b. Oct. 2, 1813, d.—all born at Sutton; Mary m. and lives at Valley Falls, R. I.; †Leonard lives at ·do.; Caroline m. lives at Woonsocket Falls, R. I.; Sarah m. and lives at Valley Falls, R. I.; Harriet b. at Oxford, Mass., lives at do.; Harrison d. The last six of this family were born at Shrewsbury, Mass.

CHILDREN OF JONATHAN, 3d, Great-grandson of Samuel, Esq.

Simon, b. Dec. 24, 1789, m. Betsey ; Polly, b. Aug. 10, 1791; Lydia, b. April 27, 1793; Jonathan, 4th, b. July 9, 1798, m.

Sarah   , and d. at S., Dec. 8, 1847; HANNAH, b. Nov. 10, 1801; ELIJAH, b. July 30, 1803; ADELINE, b. May 4, 1805, m. Nathaniel Dodge, Sept. 10, 1829, at Sutton; JASON, b. Nov. 6, 1808; ELMIRA, b. Nov. 26, 1810, d. Jan. 4, 1846, at S.; SUSANNA, b. Dec. 11, 1812. They were all born at Sutton, Mass.

CHILDREN OF ELIJAH, SON OF JONATHAN, JR.

†BENJAMIN, b. Dec. 18, 1792, at Roxbury, d. March 15, 1814, at R. ELIZABETH C., b. Nov. 24, 1794, at R., m. Nathan Griggs, Dec. 27, 1812, d. Dec. 31, 1844, at Cambridge. LUCINDA E., b. Nov. 24, 1794, at R., m. Jonathan Ford, of Cambridge. CAROLINE, b. Jan. 25, 1802, at R., d. Oct. 31, 1802. SOPHIA, b. Nov. 26, 1799, at R., m. Thomas N. Kingsbury, Jan. 7, 1827, at Boston.

CHILDREN OF JOHN, JR., GRANDSON OF JONATHAN.

JOHN, 3D, b. March 3, 1793; SALLY, b. Sept. 21, 1795; LOMIRA, b. Dec. 29, 1797, m. Stephen W. Hunt, at Sutton, June 1, 1830; POLLY, b. Feb. 19, 1800; EDWARD, b. Jan. 12, 1812; LEONARD, b. March 8, 1802, d. May 12, 1842, at S.; JAMES, b. May 13, 1805, m. Dolly   , d. Dec. 19, 1844. They were all born at Sutton, Mass.

CHILDREN OF JOSEPH, SON OF JOHN, *Son of Jonathan, Son of Samuel, Esq.*

JUDITH, b. Sept. 25, 1794, at Sutton, m. John Blanchard, Nov. 5, 1812, at S.; SILAS, b. Feb. 1, 1797, at S.; JOSEPH, JR., b. May 3, 1799, at S.

Sixth Generation.

CHILDREN OF GERRY, SON OF ABEL, JR., *Grandson of David.*

HARRIET L., b. at Shrewsbury, April 16,* 1828, lives at Cambridge port, Mass.; ABIGAIL F., b. at S., June 2, 1829, l. at C.; MARY A., b. Aug. 16, 1831, at C.; GEORGE A., b. at S., May 16, 1834, l. at C.

CHILDREN OF SIMON, SON OF JONATHAN, 3D.

SARAH ELIZABETH, b. Jan. 3, 1818, at Sutton; LOUISA MARIA, b. March 23, 1820, at S.; MARTHA ANN, b. Sept. 6, 1823, at S.; SIMON, JR., b. Dec. 16, 1828, at S.

---

* The town record is "April 15th."

CHILDREN OF JONATHAN, 4TH, *descended from Samuel, Esq.*

EDWIN A., b. June 22, 1827, at Sutton; ANN E., b. Jan. 2, 1831, at S.

CHILDREN OF JAMES, SON OF JOHN, JR.

JANE L., b. Dec. 25, 1835; JOHN L., b. Aug. 20, 1837; JAMES M., b. March 6, 1841; ANN E., b. March 10, 1843; SARAH L., d. Sept. 26, 1840. They were born at Sutton.

Seventh Generation.

CHILDREN OF DAVID T., SON OF DAVID, *Son of Abel, Jr.,* *Grandson of Samuel, Esq.*

LUCY AUGUSTA, b. Aug. 28, 1847, at Sutton; *Others,* doubtless, whose names are not known to me.

Generation Unknown.

CHILDREN OF DAVID, *whose wife was 'Phebe Dudley.'*

CALEB, b. 1804, d. Oct. 22, 1830, at Sutton; PETER, b. 1807, d. July 31, 1840, at S.; ELBRIDGE GERRY, b. 1810, d. April 12, 1834, at S.; BETSEY E., b. 1815, d. April 19, 1834, at S.; DAVID T. m. Lucy L. Wilder, Nov. 29, 1838, at S. They were born at Sutton, Mass.

CHILDREN OF PETER, AND JULIETT, HIS WIFE.

CALEB FISHER, b. Nov. 27, 1830; CHARLES H., b. March 10, 1833; SARAH P., b. Nov. 30, 1834; MARY C., b. April 13, 1836;—all born at Sutton.

CHILDREN OF EDWARD M., AND BETSEY, HIS WIFE.

MARY E., b. Nov. 16, 1839, at Sutton; EDWARD B., b. Oct. 17, 1842, at S.

CHILDREN OF JOHN, JR., AND MARY, HIS WIFE.

JOHN W., b. Nov. 30, 1840, at Sutton; MARY, b. July 26, 1844, at S.

Marriages.

SIBELLA m. Joseph Morsley, Oct. 18, 1750, at Sutton, Mass. MRS. AB-
IGAIL m. Dr. Benjamin Morse, May 25, 1735, at S. PRUDENCE m.
Ebenezer Whipple, March 25, 1736, at S. MARY m. Jonathan Eliot,
Jan. 19, 1764, at S. STEPHEN m. Rebecca Minard, July 18, 1782, at
S. HANNAH m. Asa Walker, May 30, 1787, at S. DAVID m. Hannah
Sibley, Nov. 17, 1789, at S. DAVID m. Rachel Chase, Nov. 6, 1791, at S.
POLLY m. Samuel Dwinel, July 15, 1793, at S. POLLY m. Jacob Brig-
ham, Dec. 16, 1793, at S. SALLY, m. Salmon Waters, Oct. 10, 1798,
at S. DAVID m. Phebe Dudley, Feb. 18, 1804, at S. ABIGAIL m. Simeon
Gould, Dec. 3, 1797, at S. SALLY m. Reuben M. Knight, April 18, 1813,
at S. MARY m. Abraham Chase, Nov. 20, 1814, at S. PATTY, of Dou-
glas, m. Asa Putman, Jr., Nov. 28, 1815, at S. SALLY m. Welcome
Adams, Dec. 11, 1820, at S. PETER, 2d, m. Juliett Robinson, Dec. 2,
1829, at S. RACHEL m. Rufus Marble, July 15, 1823, at S. EDWARD
M. m. Betsey S. Bartlett, March 27, 1839, at S. JOHN, JR. m. Mary
Woodbury, Jan. 1, 1841, at S. SUSAN m. Sumner Putnam, July 1,
1840, at S. HANNAH m. Josiah Adams, April, 1827. BENJAMIN m.
Mary A. R———, who d. at S., May 23, 1844.

Deaths.

JOSEPH d. at Sutton, Mass. March 30, 1799. MRS. HANNAH, widow
of David, d. at S., Oct. 19, 1816. WILLIAM d. at S., Nov. 18, 1822.

VARIOUS FAMILIES AND INDIVIDUALS.

WILLIAM DUDLEY emigrated from England, and arrived at Boston, Mass., in 1637. After remaining there during one winter, he proceeded to Guilford, then in New Haven Colony, now in the State of Connecticut, where he settled in 1638.

From him, have descended quite a numerous posterity, among whom there have been and are at the present time many persons of distinguished abilities and accomplishments.

LEWIS J. DUDLEY, A. M., of Hartford, Ct., WILLIAM C. DUDLEY, of Guilford, Ct., and GEO. A. DUDLEY, of Ellenville, N. Y., are of this branch of the family.

[Another family in Conn.]

CAPT. JOHN E. DUDLEY, seaman, afterwards school master, immigrated to Conn. from Ireland about 1746, and settled in the town of Wallingford. He m. Lois Brocket, of Wallingford, and d. about 1828, in the State of New York, aged about 90 years.

THE CHILDREN OF CAPT. JOHN E.

JEDEDIAH m. Lucy Plumbe, of Wallingford, and died about 1797; MARY.

THE CHILDREN OF JEDEDIAH.

JOHN E. m. a lady of Wallingford; CALEB m. a lady of W.; RANSOM; ELIAS m. Laura Preston, of W., l. in 1848, in Cheshire, Ct.; ISAAC; SALLY d. in early life; LUCY d. in early life; PAMELIA; ROXANA m. and had a family; SARAH.

CHILDREN OF JOHN E., Son of Jedediah.

Ebenezer; Goodrich; John E., Jr.; Clarissa,—who are all married, and have families in Connecticut.

CHILDREN OF CALEB, Son of Jedediah.

Sophronia; Delight; who are married, and have families.

CHILDREN OF ELIAS, Son of Jedediah.

Joseph, b. 1823; George E., b. 1827; Charles W., b. 1835; Samuel, b. 1837, all at Cheshire, Ct.; Maria F., b. at Middleton, 1816, d. 1838, at Cheshire; Mary A., b. at Wallingford, 1819, m. 1841; Harriet, b. at Cheshire, 1821, m. 1842; Caroline, b. at C., 1825.

[At Beverly, Mass.]

Mr. Jonathan Dudley and Miss Hannah Carter, both of Beverly, published their intention of marriage, April 4, 1795.

CHILDREN OF JOSIAH DUDLEY, and Sally, his wife.

Allen W., born May 20, 1838. Lucretia V., b. Dec. 23, 1825. Josiah F, b. Oct. 27, 1831. Harriet M., b. Aug. 3, 1840.

[At Orange and Littleton, Ms.]

Mr. Warren Dudley m. Miss Harriet C. Bishop, May, 1848; Stephen Dudley lived at Littleton, Mass. in 1767. He was probably a son of Samuel, Esq., son of Francis, 1st, of Concord. Samuel, Esq., also lived here at this time.

[In Philadelphia reside,]

George Dudley, manufacturer, and Jacob Dudley, carpenter.

[Dudleys in New York city.]

Abraham A., Gilman, Jonas G., Charles H., Richard, Samuel B., George V., William, William Jr.; Jonas G., Jr., Thomas C., and others.

[At Weston.]

Benjamin Dudley, lived at Weston, Mass., in 1782.

[At Stockbridge]

Wright Dudley, merchant, lived at Stockbridge, Mass., in 1793.

[At Newport, R. I.]

CHARLES DUDLEY, who was a Collector of Customs at Newport, R. I. in 1776, being a Royalist, embarked with the British Army at Boston, for Halifax.

[At Boston.]

STEPHEN DUDLEY, mariner, formerly of London, Eng., late of Boston, N. E., died at the latter place in 1719.

[In Vermont.]

REV. JOHN DUDLEY, who resides in Quechee Village, Vt., married Abigail P. Wade, of Ipswich, Mass. His father resides in Lynden, White Side, Co., Ill.

[In England.]

SIR HENRY BATE DUDLEY, whose original name was *Bate*, was b. in 1745, at Fenny Compton, d. 1824.

In the records of the Parish of Bromley, Eng., occurs the following entrance, "Joseph, Benjamin, Rachel, Children of John Dudley, bap. Oct. 17, 1724, buried Oct. 20, 1724."

[At Stoneplace.]

ELEANOR, dau. and only heir of Dudley, of Stoneplace, Co. of Kent. What Dudley of Stoneplace?

[In Virginia.]

BISHOP DUDLEY, supposed to have been born in England, m. Rebecca Ward, and died in 1788, in the State of N. Carolina. His brother, William Dudley, is thought to have m. Miss Ward, a sister of Rebecca Ward, mentioned above.

[In North Carolina.]

THE CHILDREN OF BISHOP DUDLEY, were CHRISTOPHER, born 1763, died 1828, in N. C. ‡BISHOP, JR., died 1790. EDWARD; ‡JOHN; CREED; ‡GUILFORD; ANN; MARGARET.

THE CHILDREN OF CHRISTOPHER, SON OF BISHOP.

‡ROBERT; ‡CHRISTOPHER, JR.; EDWARD BISHOP; ‡POLLY; NANCY had posterity; JOHN had posterity.

THE CHILDREN OF EDWARD BISHOP, SON OF CHRISTOPHER, *Son of Bishop.*

CHRISTOPHER; WILLIAM; HENRY; EDWARD; ELIZA ANN; JANE; MARGARET. Of whom *Edward*, alone, has deceased.

14

[In Virginia and Kentucky.]

ROBERT DUDLEY, whose father died several years before the commencement of the Revolutionary War, was the eldest of five brothers, viz: ROBERT, AMBROSE, PETER, JAMES and WILLIAM, all minors at the time of their father's death. *He* died soon after the *Battle of Brandywine*, of wounds received in that conflict, where he served as Lieutenant.

AMBROSE, who was a captain in the Virginia line, emigrated to Kentucky in early life, and died near Lexington, in 1826.

MAJ. PETER lived and died (several years since) on the paternal estate, near Fredericksburg, Va. JAMES died in Bourbon Co., Ky., in 1808.

COL. WILLIAM was slain at the head of his regiment, at Fort Meigs, May, 1813.

DR. B. W. DUDLEY, of Lexington, Ky., and, I think, Col. Dudley, of Cincinnati, Ohio, are sons of Capt. Ambrose D.

W. A. DUDLEY, of Lexington, Ky., and ED. DUDLEY, belong to this branch of the family.

[At Springfield.]

HUGH DUDLEY, of Springfield, Mass., a slave to Mr. Edward Pynchon, m. Mary Copsey, in 1656.

[At Douglas.]

PAUL DUDLEY died in Douglas, Mass.; his children were DAVID, who m. Hannah Walker, at Sutton, Dec. 16, 1810, d. 1829, at D.; JOHN; WILLIAM; WILLARD; DOROTHY; HARRIET. *David had a son* GEORGE R., who resides in Cincinnati, Ohio. The children of George R., are EUGENE, EMMA, and ANNA.

HON. CHARLES E. DUDLEY. late of Albany, deceased, was a few years since a senator in Congress from New York.

[In Ireland.]

MICHAEL DUDLEY d. in Dublin; his only son, WILLIAM, b. Dec. 1806, at Dublin, came to Boston, Mass., 1819, m. Ann E. Moran, and lives at Boston.

THE CHILDREN OF WILLIAM DUDLEY.

ELIZA; ALEXIS; LOUISA A.; WILLIAM F.; JANE A., CORDELIA M., Twins; CHARLES J. C.; JOSEPH V.; CLEMENT J.; ANN J.; MARY I.

[From a London Newspaper.]

"A gentleman by the name of William Dudley, who lived in Richmond street, London, died intestate in 1813, leaving consols unclaimed —20.—up to this date, 1847."

[In England.]

Rev. John Dudley, A. M., was living in 1729; Joshua Dudley was living in 1772.

Ann Dudley, dau. and heiress of John D., Esq., of Stoke, Newington, m. Sir Francis Popham, Kt., of Littlecot, member of Qu. Elizabeth's Parliament and all those of James I. and Charles I.

This John Dudley is said to have been a grandson of Thomas, son of " Edward " lord Dudley. Perhaps it should be written " Edmund " [De Sutton] lord Dudley.

Ann, dau. of John Dudley, m. Robt. Hawley, of Ore and Gestling, Co. of Sussex.

GRADUATES BY THE NAME OF DUDLEY.

[At Harvard, Cambridge, Mass.]
THOMAS, son of Rev. Samuel, in 1651, A. M.
JOSEPH, son of Gov. Thomas, in 1665, A. M.
THOMAS, son of Gov. Joseph, in 1685, A. M.
PAUL, son of   do.   in 1690, A. M., Tutor.
WILLIAM, son of   do.   in 1704, A. M.
THOMAS, son of Col. William, in 1750, A. M.
JOSEPH, son of   do.   in 1751, A. M.
NICHOLAS, son of Trueworthy, in 1767, A. M.

[At Yale, New Haven, Ct.]
ASAHEL, in 1769.
LEWIS J., in 1838, A. M. Tutor.
MARTIN, in 1839.

[At Dartmouth, Hanover, N. H.]
ELIAS, in 1788, A. M.
ELBRIDGE GERRY, son of Hon. Moses, in 1839.

[At Western Reserve, Hudson, Ohio.]
ROSWELL, in 1833.

[At University of North Carolina.]
WILLIAM H. H., in 1840.

[At Christ Church, Oxford, Eng.]
JOHN, Feb. 3, 1776, A. M.

[At Jesus, Cambridge, Eng.]
SAMUEL, in 1666, A. B.
JOHN, in 1715, A. B.

[At Emanuel, Cambridge.]
THOMAS, A. B. in 1626, and A. M. in 1630.
WILLIAM, in 1682, A. M.

[At Clare Hall, Cambridge.]
JOHN, in 1785, A. B.
CHARLES, in 1823.

DUDLEY LINEAGE OF OTHER NAMES.

ASHBURNHAM,* THOMAS m. ELIZABETH DUDLEY.
Their Son,
Thomas m.   ;
Their Son,
Laurence m. Eva, dau. of Richard Adams, Esq., of Herietsham, Co. of Kent, and widow of John Levet, Esq.
Their Grandson,
Laurence m. Bridget Fleetwood, dau. of Sir George F., of the Vache, Co. of Bucks, l. at Bromham.
Their eldest Son,
Denny, M. P., Bart., m. 1st, Frances Ashburnham, dau. of John A., Esq.
Their only surviving Daughter,
Bridget m. the Rev. Mr. Bradshaw, Rector of Pett and Vicar of Gosling, Co. of Sussex; he m. 2dly, Ann Watkins, dau. of David W., and d. 1697.
His Children,
‡Sir William, M. P., d. Nov. 7, 1775; Sir Charles m.   .
The Son of Sir Charles,
Sir William, Bishop of Chichester, m. Margaret Pelham, dau. of Thomas P., Esq., 1766.

ALLEN, DR. WILLIAM H., *of Maine*, m. ANN B. WEBSTER.
Their Children,
Lucy W.; Ebenezer W.; Nathan W.; Anna M.

ATKINS, THOMAS, *of Mt. Vernon, Me.*, m. BETSEY DUDLEY.
Their Children,
Rev. Thomas m. Lucinda Fairbanks, lives at Canaan, Me.; Joseph m. 1st, Eliza Blanchard; 2d, Eunice Carr, lives at New Sharon, Me.; Rev. John W. m. Elizabeth Pierce.

---

* The seat of this family was Bromham Park, Sussex.

AVERY, WILLIAM, *of Maine,* m. SUSAN H. WEBSTER.
Their Children,
Martha A., b. Dec. 16, 1842 ;   Maria C., b. Aug. 26, 1844 ;   William S., b. Dec. 30, 1845.

BAILEY, CAPT. SAMUEL, *of Maine,* m. Catharine Dudley.
Their Children,
Paul D., b. June 28, 1803, d. Dec. 5, 1813 ;   Charles, b. March 10, 1805, m. Mary J. Ring, Dec. 9, 1834, who was b. March 31, 1807 ; Nancy D. b. July 20, 1807, m. Col. Richard H. Bartlett, July 7, 1827, and d. Oct. 6, 1827 ; Col. B. was b. 1799, and d. Aug. 29, 1841 ;   Lucy, b. Sept. 17, 1808, m. 1st, Nathan Winslow, of Milford ; 2d, John Treat ;   Lucretia, b. Aug. 5, 1810, m. Capt. Alexander Woodward ;   Martha D., b. Sept. 6, 1812, m. Daniel A. Cressy, Sept. 1, 1831, who was b. March 19, 1804, and d. Oct. 22, 1846 ; William, b. July 29, 1814, m. Olivia C. Dudley, dau. of John D., March 26, 1838, who was b. Oct. 5, 1817 ;   Catharine, b. June 27, 1816, m. Amos Bailey, Jr., Oct. 8, 1835, who was b. Jan. 31, 1814 ; Daniel, b. Sept. 21, 1818, m. Mary W. Woodward, Oct. 27, 1842, who was b. May 28, 1817, and d. June 4, 1846 ;   Samuel b. Aug. 2, 1820, d. Dec. 30, 1820 ;   Paul D., b. Aug. 2, 1820, d. Jan. 21 1821.

BAILEY, WILLIAM, m. OLIVIA C. DUDLEY.
Their Daughter,
Caroline E., b. May 18, 1839.

BAILEY, AMOS, JR. m. CATHARINE BAILEY.
Their Children,
Emily A., b. May 23, 1836 ;   Ira F., b. April 4, 1838 ;   Allen B., b. March 3, 1840 ;   Samuel F., b. April 13, 1842, d. May 22, 1842 ; Emma F., b. Aug. 26, 1843, d. July 19, 1845 ;   Francis E., b. July 7, 1845.

BAILEY, DAVID, m. MARY W. WOODWARD.
Their Children,
Sarah A., b. May 17, 1843, d. March 9, 1844 ;   Warren B., b. July 28, 1844.

BAILEY, CHARLES, ESQ., m. MARY J. RING.
Their Children,
Catharine, b. April 6, 1835 ;   William C., b. July 22, 1836 ;   Lucretia W., b. Aug. 19, 1838 ;   Charles R., b. May 15, 1843 ;   Mary E., b. April 25, 1845 ;   Woodbury, b. Nov. 2, 1846.

BARTLET, Col. Richard H., *of Maine*, m. Nancy D. Bailey.
Their Daughter,
Catharine F., b. July 21, 1827, d. Sept. 27, 1827.

BARTLET, Israel, *of New Hampshire*, m. Love Hall.
Their Children,
Joseph H., lives in Massachusetts ; Sarah m. 1st, Col. Winbourne
Adams ; 2d, Col. Hubbard ; Hon. Israel lives at Haverhill, Mass. ;
Mary m. Gen. Henry Dearborn ; Josiah lives at Lee, N. H. ;
Judge Thomas lives at Nottingham, N. H.

BIXBY, Benjamin, *of Massachusetts*, m. Margaret Peabody.
Their Children,
Sarah, b. Aug. 19, 1771 ; Joseph, b. April 28, 1773 ; Elizabeth,
b. Aug. 18, 1779 ; Daniel, b. Jan. 19, 1781, and d. Jan. 24, 1836 ;
Margaret, b. May 30, 1783 ; Asa, b. July 24, 1786.

BIXBY, Daniel, m. Sarah Towne, *April* 16, 1807.
Their Children,
Julia ; Elbridge S. ; Daniel ; Lucinda ; George, and Charles P.

BIXBY, Benjamin, *of Topsfield, Mass.*, m. Ann Bradstreet.
Their Children,
Dudley ; Asa ; George ; Sarah ; Benjamin, b. Jan. 2, 1747, m.
Margaret Peabody, Oct. 9, 1770.

BEAN, Reuben, *of New Hampshire*, m. Joanna Dudley.
Their Children,
Moses m. Mary Hook ; Dudley m. Susan Robinson ; Reuben, Jr.
m. Sally Ward ; Joseph m. Abigail Cilley ; Susanna m. 1st, Jacob
Quimby ; 2d, Mr. Lucy, of Deerfield, N. H. ; Mary m. John Robin-
son, of Candia, N. H. ; Elizabeth m. Enoch James, of Deerfield, N. H.

BENNOCH, Josiah, *of Maine*, m. Lucy Webster.
Their Children,
John E. ; Daniel W. ; Charles W.

BLAISDELL, Richard, *of Maine*, m. Lucy F. Dudley.
Their Children,
David, b. Oct. 22, 1828 ; John, b. April 22, 1830 ; Charles b.
Feb. 12, 1832, d. Aug. 26, 1833 ; Nancy, b. Dec. 29, 1833 ;
Thomas B., b. July 1, 1836 ; Richard H., b. July 27, 1838 ; Ann
M., b. June 27, 1840 ; Mary E., b. July 17, 1842 ; Lucy, b. Jan.
12, 1844 ; Daniel, b. Oct. 4, 1847, d. March 31, 1848.

BLANCHARD, Capt. Alexander, m. Sally Dudley.
Their Children,
Mary Ann T. m. Thomas Cushing, of Weymouth, Mass.; Elizabeth T. m. Joseph Blanchard, of Freeman, Me.; Alexander; Marcellus; Horatio N.;—all born at Freeman, Me.

BRADSTREET, Gov. Simon,* m. Ann Dudley, *Poetess.*§
Their Children,
Hon. Samuel, sometime fellow of Harvard College, and 1670, a Representative of Andover, Mass.; Rev. Simon, b. 1640, grad. at Harvard College, in 1660, settled at New London, 1670, d. at New London, 1685; Col. Dudley, b. perhaps, 1648, m. Ann Price, Nov. 12, 1673, d. at Andover, 1706; John, b. July 22, 1652, at Andover, m. Sarah Perkins, dau. of Rev. William P., of Topsfield, June 11,

---

* Gov. B. was born at Horbling, Lincolnshire, Eng, March, 1603. His second wife was a daughter of Emanuel Downing, and sister of Sir George D. He died at Salem, Mass., March 27, 1697.

§ IN REFERENCE TO HER CHILDREN.

I had eight birds hatched in one nest,
Four cocks there were, and hens the rest;
I nursed them up with pain and care,
For cost nor labor did I spare,
Till, at the last, they felt their wing,
Mounted the trees, and learned to sing;
Chief of the brood then took his flight
To regions far, and left me quite;
My mournful chirps I after send,
Till he return, or I do end.
Leave not my nest, thy dam and shire,
Go back, and sing amidst this choir.
A second bird did take her flight,
And, with her mate, flew out of sight.
Southward they both their course did bend,
And seasons twain they there did spend;
Till, after blown by southern gales,
They northward steered with filléd sails.
A prettier bird was no where seen,
Along the beach, among the treen;
I have a third, of color white,
On whom I place no small delight,
Coupled with mate loving and true,
Hath also bid her dam adieu;

1677,* d. Jan. 11, 1718, at Topsfield, Mass.; ~~Ann m. Mr. Wiggin, of Exeter, N. H.~~; Dorothy m. Rev. Seaborn Cotton, of Hampton, N. H., June 25, 1654, d. Feb. 26, 1672, at H.; Hannah m. Hon. Andrew Wiggin, of Exeter, N. H., June 14, 1659; Mercy m. Maj. Nathaniel Wade, Oct. 31, 1672.

BRADSTREET, THE CHILDREN OF REV. SIMON.
Rev. Simon, Jr., b. 1669, probably at New London, Ct , grad. Harvard College, 1693, m.   , d. at Charlestown, Dec. 31, 1741. *There were, doubtless, others.*

BRADSTREET, Col. DUDLEY, m. ANN PRICE.
Their Children,
Dudley, b. April 27, 1678, at Andover; Margaret, b. Feb. 19, 1673; Ann, b. Nov. 5, 1681, d. Nov. 12, 1681.

BRADSTREET, JOHN, *of Topsfield, Mass.* m. SARAH PERKINS.
Their Children,
Simon, b. April 14, 1682, at Topsfield, Mass., m. Elizabeth Capen, dau. of Rev. Joseph C., of Topsfield, Oct. 12, 1711; John, b Jan. 30, 1693, at T., m. Rebecca   ; Margaret, b. Nov. 27, 1696, at T.; Samuel, b. Aug. 4, 1699, at T., m. Sarah Clarke, April 3, 1722.

The Children of Rev. Simon Bradstreet, Jr.
Mary m. Rev. Hull Abbot, July 27, 1731, at Charlestown, Mass., d. May 10, 1763; Rev. Simon grad. at Harvard College, 1728, d. Oct. 5, 1771, at Marblehead; Samuel m. Sarah ———, d. 1755.

And where Aurora first appears,
She now hath perched to spend her years;
And one unto the college flew,
To chat among the learned crew;
Ambition moves still in his breast,
That he might chant above the rest,
Striving for more, than to do well,
That nightingales he might excel.
My fifth, whose down is yet scarce gone,
Is 'mongst the shrubs and bushes flown,
And, as his wings increase in strength,
On higher boughs he 'll perch at length.
My other three still, with me, nest,
Until they 've grown, then, as the rest,
Or here or there they 'll take their flight,
As is ordained, so shall they light.

June 23, 1656.   ANNE BRADSTREET.

* They were married by Maj. Gen. Daniel Dennison.

The Children of Samuel and Sarah Bradstreet,
Sarah, bap. Feb, 10, 1740 ; Sarah, 2d, bap. May 24, 1741, at
Charlestown ; Lucy, bap. June 12, 1747, at C ; Mary, bap. April 7,
1751, at C.

BRADSTREET, SIMON, m. ELIZABETH CAPEN.
Their Children,
Simon, b. April 21, 1714, m. Miss Flint ; Mercy b. Nov. 27, 1728,
m. Mr. Stone ; Margaret, b. April 24, 1720, m. Mr. Andrews ; Mary,
b. May 10, 1731, m. Elisha Wildes ; Lucy, b. Nov. 25, 1724, m.
Robert Andrews, 1776 ; Elizabeth, b. Aug. 28, 1712, m. Joseph
Peabody, of Topsfield, Nov. 2, 1729, and d. Dec. 31, 1751 ; Dr.
Joseph, b. May 13, 1727, m. Abby Fuller, of Middleton ; John, b.
March 2, 1718, m. Elizabeth Fisk, of Wenham ; Dudley, b. May
27, 1716 ; Priscilla, b. Sept. 27, 1722.

BRADSTREET, JOHN, m. ELIZABETH FISK, Jan. 13, 1742.
Their Children,
Priscilla, b. Jan. 8, 1745, m. John Killam, of Boxford, June 12,
1764 ; Mary, b. Dec. 22, 1748 ; Mehitable, b. June 2, 1751 ;
Huldah, b. April 15, 1754 ; Lucy, b. March 27, 1758 ; Eunice,
b. Aug. 16, 1760, m. Benjamin Emerson, March 25, 1783 ; Capt.
Dudley, b. Oct. 8, 1765, m. Polly Porter, of Danvers, Sept. 29,
1789, d. April 23, 1833 ; Elizabeth m. John Gould, 1769 ; Sarah
b. Feb. 1, 1756, m. Daniel Gould.

BRADSTREET, JOHN, SON OF JOHN, m. REBECCA ———.
Their Children,
Sarah, b. March 8, 1729-30, Boanerges, b. July 1, 1733.

BRADSTREET, SAMUEL, SON OF JOHN, m. SARAH CLARKE.
Their Children,
Ann, b. Oct. 23, 1724 ; Sarah b. Feb. 4, 1726-7 ; Samuel, b.
March 8, 1729, m. Ruth Lamson, April 5, 1763 ; Elijah, b. Aug. 8,
1731 ; Eunice, b. April 15, 1733 ; Asa, b. April 20, 1736.

BRADSTREET, SAMUEL, SON OF SAMUEL, m. RUTH LAMSON.
Their Children,
Samuel, b. Jan. 2, 1764, m. Matilda Foster, April 14, 1785 ;
Ruth, b. March 8, 1766, m. Billy Emerson, of Topsfield, May 8,
1791 ; Elijah, b. July 4, 1767, m. Phebe Ingalls, of Andover ; Asa,
b. May 29, 1769, m. Abigail Balch, of Topsfield, Nov. 30, 1790 ;
John, b. Dec. 9, 1771, m. Mehitable Balch, Jan. 9, 1793 ; Moses,
b. Aug. 26, 1773, m. Lydia Peabody, May 7, 1795.

BRADSTREET, Capt. Dudley, m. Polly Porter.
Their Children,
Col. Porter, b. Dec. 1, 1789, at Topsfield, m. Mehitable Bradstreet, April 8, 1812, lives at T., upon the farm formerly owned by Gov. Simon B., it having remained in the possession of the family ever since his time ; Maj. John, b. Oct. 8, 1792, m. Sarah Rea, April 23, 1826 ; †Dudley, b. Aug. 16, 1796, d. Sept. 25, 1832 ; Mary, b. Aug. 10, 1798, m. Samuel Peabody, of Boxford, April 30, 1818 ; Joseph, b. Nov. 1, 1801, m. Abigail Shaw, of Beverly ; Elizabeth P., b. Jan. 11, 1803, m. Silas Cochran, Dec. 20, 1846 ; Albert G., b. May 19, 1805, m. Lydia B. Stearns, of Boston, April 5, 1836 ; Rev. Thomas J.,*. b. April 7, 1807, grad. at Yale College, m. Amanda Thomas, of Plymouth, Conn. ; Sarah, b. March 7, 1812, m. Ahira H. Putnam, of Danvers, Oct. 8, 1834 ; †Jonathan, b. Oct. 1, 1808, d. April 6, 1842 ; Lydia, b. Nov. 30, 1813, m. Stephen White, of South Hadley, Mass., May 18, 1847.

BRADSTREET, Col. Porter, m. Mehitable Bradstreet.
Their Children,
Mehitable, b. Sept. 5, 1812, d. Aug. 10, 1825 ; Hannah P., b. March 5, 1823, m. Humphrey Balch, of Topsfield, April 10, 1842.

BRADSTREET, Maj. John, m. Sarah Rea.
Their Children,
Dudley, b. July 6, 1827 ; John, b. April 25, 1829 ; Israel R., b. Dec. 23, 1830 ; Harrison P., b. March 31, 1836 ; Sarah R., b. April 30, 1839.

BRADSTREET, Joseph, m. Abigail Shaw.
Their Children,
Mary ; Horatio.

BRADSTREET, Albert G., m. Lydia B. Stearns.
Their Children,
Harriet J. ; Sarah W. ; Lydia P. ; Elizabeth S.

BRADSTREET, Samuel, Son of Samuel, m. Matilda Foster.
Their Children,
Abigail, b. Dec. 31, 1786 ; Samuel, b. Aug. 26, 1787 ; Ruth, b. Nov. 4, 1791 ; Nathaniel, b. Sept. 20, 1795 ; Moses, b. July 26, 1800.

---

* He has a son, Thomas Dudley Bradstreet.

BRADSTREET, Elijah, m. Phebe Ingalls.
Their Children,
Eliza; Elijah; Stephen; Phebe; Ruth; Ruby.

BRADSTREET, Asa, m. Abigail Balch.
Their Children,
William, b. June 26, 1792, m. Eunice Perkins, of Topsfield, April, 1814; Asa, b. Sept. 8, 1793.

BRADSTREET, John, m. Mehitable Balch.
Their Children,
Mehitable, b. March 29, 1793; Cornelius, b. Oct. 30, 1796; Ruth, b. Feb. 16, 1799; Cynthia, b. Nov. 1802; Josiah, b. Sept. 25, 1804; John, b. Nov. 11, 1811.

BRADSTREET, Moses, m. Lydia Peabody.
Their Children,
Lydia, b. Jan. 8, 1796, m. Nehemiah Perkins, of Topsfield, May 4, 1817; Phebe, b. Oct. 10, 1798; Cynthia d. young; Eunice, b. Aug. 23, 1801.

BRADSTREET, William, m. Eunice Perkins.
Their Children,
Abigail B., b. Oct. 30, 1814; Asa, b. Sept. 1, 1816; Marietta, b. Aug. 29, 1818; Lydia, b. Aug. 29, 1820; William, b. Jan. 5, 1823; Fanny, b. Jan. 14, 1825; Elijah, b. March 8, 1829; Louisa K., b. March 7, 1832; Moses, b. June 14, 1834; Alonzo A., b. April 29, 1839;—all born at Topsfield.

BUCK, Daniel, *of Wethersfield,* m. Sarah Saltonstall.
Their Children,
Gurdon m. Susanna Manwaring; Daniel m. 1st, Julia Mitchell, dau. of Judge M., of Wethersfield, Ct.; and 2d, Elizabeth Belden; Charles m. Catherine Bradford, of N. Y.; Winthrop m. 1st, Miss Parsons; 2d, Eunice Moseley; Dudley m. 1st, Hetty Hempstead; 2d, Martha Adams.

BUCK, CHILDREN OF GURDON.
David m. Matilda Hall; Gurdon m. Henrietta Wolff, of Geneva, Switzerland; Charles D.; Daniel; Sarah; Edward; George; Henry; Elizabeth m. John Auchincloss, of N. Y.; Rebecca C.

CHILD, Richards, m. Elizabeth Richards.
Their Children,
Elizabeth, b. July 24, 1813, at Boston, m. Dr. Abel Ball, dentist, l., 1848, at Boston ; Henry, b. July 17, 1815, at B., d. April 6, 1816 ; Henry, 2d, b. July 25, 1816, at B., m. Mrs. Freeman, and died at Hillsborough, Ill.

COIT, Elisha, m. Rebecca Manwaring.
Their Children,
Martha M. ; Mary Ann m. 1st, Rev. Henry Blatchford, of Salem, Mass. ; 2d, Samuel Hubbard, LL. D., of Boston ; William D. ; Susanna M. m. Thomas Adams, merchant, of Boston ; Sarah L. m. Charles Scudder, merchant, of Boston ; Gurdon S. m. Mary Ann Berwick.

COTTON, Rev. Seaborn, *of Hampton,* m. Dorothy Bradstreet.
Their Children,
Dorothy, b. Nov. 11, 1656, m. Col. Joseph Smith, of Hampton, N. H. ; Rev. John, b. May 8, 1658, was a minister at Hampton, m. Ann Lake, dau. of Capt. Thomas L., of Boston ; Sarah, b. Feb. 22, 1660, d. in infancy, April 1, 1660 ; Ann, b. Aug. 22, 1661, m. Mr. Johnson ; Sarah, b. July 2, 1663, m. Richard Peirce, of Boston, Aug. 27, 1680, d. Aug. 2, 1690 ; Elizabeth, b. Aug. 13, 1665, m. Rev. William Williams, of Hatfield, d. 1698 ; Mercy, b. Nov. 3, 1666, m. Capt. Peter Tufts, of Medford, d. June 18, 1715 ; Abiah, b. April 5, 1669 ; Maria, b. April 22, 1670, m. 1st, Mr. Atwater ; 2d, Samuel Partridge, d. 1729.

COTTON, Rev. John, m. Ann Lake.
Their Children,
Mary, b. Nov. 5, 1689, m. Rev. John Whiting, of Concord, Mass., d. May 29, 1731 ; John, b. Sept. 5, 1687, d. Sept. 8, 1689 ; Dorothy, b. July 16, 1693, m. Rev. Nathaniel Gookin, of Hampton, Dec. 21, 1710, d. May 20, 1748, at Kingston, N. H. ; Thomas, b. Oct. 28, 1695, l. at Brookline, Mass. ; Anna, b. Nov. 13, 1697 ; Simon, b. Dec. 21, 1701 ; Samuel and Lydia d. young.

CRESSY, Daniel A., *of Maine,* m. Martha D. Bailey.
Their Children,
Emily F., b. Feb. 21, 1833, d. May 27, 1833 ; Ellen L., b. Nov. 14, 1834 ; Daniel W., b. July 1, 1837, d. April 26, 1837 ; Martha A., b. July 1, 1839 ; David B., b. March 29, 1841 ; Daniel F., b. Feb. 7, 1846.

DENNISON, MAJ. GEN. DANIEL,* *of Ipswich*, m. PATIENCE DUDLEY.
Their Children,
John, who m., and left posterity ;   Elizabeth m. Dr. John Rogers,
and left posterity ; Dr. R. d. July 2, 1684, aged 53.

DENNISON, JOHN, m.
Their Children,
John, who left posterity ;   Martha.

DODGE, JOHN, *of Beverley, Massachusetts*, m. MARY BRADSTREET,
dau. of John and Elizabeth B., Jan. 31, 1780.
Their Children,
William m. Miss Patch, of Hamilton ;   Mary m. Henry Nichols.

EMERSON, BENJAMIN, *of Massachusetts*, m. EUNICE BRADSTREET.
Their Children,
Benjamin, Jr., b. Jan. 10, 1785, m. Miss Balch ;   Mehitable, b.
Nov. 16, 1786, m. Samuel Burtlebank ;   Lucy, b. Feb. 24, 1790,
m. Mr. Davis ;   Bradstreet, b. July 4, 1793 ;   Elizabeth B., b. July
25, 1799.

EMERSON, BILLY, *of Topsfield*, m. RUTH BRADSTREET.
Their Children,
Lydia ;   Ruth ;   Eliza ;   Thomas.

EMERY, NOAH, *of New Hampshire*, m. JOANNA PERRYMAN.
Their Children,
John, b. March 20, 1746, m. Margaret Gookin.§ dau. of Rev. Nathl.
G., of Northwood, and d. 1787, at sea ;   Noah, Esq., b. Nov. 10,
1748, m. Jane Hale, who was b. May 10, 1751, and he d. Jan. 1817 ;
Elizabeth, b. Jan. 13, 1750, m. Col. Samuel Folsom ;   Nicholas, b.
June 20, 1756 ;   †Joanna, b. Sept. 20, 1758, m. Samuel B. Stevens ;
Richard, b. Oct. 24, 1762, m. Liberty Hale, who was b. April 14,
1766, and d. abroad ;   Theresa, b. April 4, 1761, m. Dr. Joseph
Orne ;   †Margaret, b. Oct. 15, 1772.

EMERY, JOHN, m. MARGARET GOOKIN.
Their Children,
Hannah T., b. March 7, 1771, m. Benjamin Abbot, LL. D., of
Exeter, N. H., and she d. Dec. 6, 1793 ;   Robert, b. Sept. 20,
1773, m. 1st, Eunice Orne ; 2d, Sarah Barnard ; 3d, Mary Lyman.

---

* Maj. Gen D. died at Ipswich, Mass., Sept 20, 1682.
§ This lady was b. Aug. 11, 1745.

EMERY, Noah, m. Jane Hale.
Their Children,

†Mary H.; Betsey, d. young; Judge Nicholas, b. Sept. 4, 1776, grad. at Dart. Coll. 1795. m. Ann T. Gilman, dau. of Gov. John T. Gilman; John, b. Oct., 1780, m. 1st, Deborah Webb, Jan., 1802; 2d, Mary Rand; Noah, b. Dec. 30, 1782, m. Elizabeth Folsom, 1811, d. Dec., 1812; Jane, b. 1788, d. 1799; Elizabeth P. m. Gideon L. Soule, Principal of Phillips' Exeter Academy.

FELLOWS, John W., m. Sally Dudley.
Their Children,

George F., d. in infancy at Roxbury; †George, b. at Roxbury, d. at R., aged 40 years; Mary, b. at R., d. in childhood.

FOLSOM, Col. Samuel, *of New Hampshire*, m. Elizabeth Emery.
Their Children,

Ann m. Joseph Tilton, Esq.; Elizabeth m. 1st, Noah Emery; 2d, Rev. Isaac Hurd, of Exeter, N. H.

GILBERT,* Spencer, m. Nancy Dudley.
Their Children,

Rebecca B. m. Tristram Norton, of Kingfield, Me.; Harrison P.; Mary Ann m. Rev. Reuben B. Curtis; Hannah H. m. Irason P. Landers, of Kingfield; Sarah D., d. in youth; William S.; Joseph S. A.; Eliza A.; Cornelius W.; Charles F.;—all born at Kingfield, Me.

GOULD, Daniel, *of Massachusetts*, m. Sarah Bradstreet, Jan. 31, 1778.
Their Children,

Sarah m. Caleb Warner, of Salem; Priscilla m. Mr. Sprague, of S., Cashier of Naumkeag Bank; Asenath m. John Perley, of Salem; Daniel m. Lydia Batchelder, of Boxford; Mehitable m. Rev. Mr. Blanchard.

GREELY, Joseph, *who was born October* 19, 1715, m. Elizabeth Dudley, *who died May* 27, 1809, *at Gilmanton, N. H. Mr. Greely died June* 5, 1799.

They had several children, whose posterity reside mostly in New Hampshire.

HARDIE, Samuel, *of Exeter, N H.*, m. Mary Dudley, 2d. ·
Their Children,

Biley; Theophilus.

---

* He was the son of Rev. Nathaniel Gilbert, who was born at Kingston, Mass.

HARTHON, ELI, *of Maine*, m. HANNAH W. DUDLEY.
Their Children,
Solomon, b. Feb. 22, 1812, m. Julia A. Field, of Sidney, Me., Feb. 20, 1845; Paul D., b. Nov. 27, 1813, m. Loantha Wyman, Dec. 29, 1847; Miss W. was born Aug. 12, 1827; Martha, b. Dec. 4, 1815, m. Samuel Orcutt, Oct. 17, 1833; Mr. O. was born Aug. 19, 1805; Matilda D., b. Nov. 2, 1817, m. William T. Willey, who was b. 1808, and d. 1844; Rebecca, b. Nov. 30, 1819, d. March 5, 1841; Eunice, b. April 8, 1822, d. Feb. 6, 1846; Catharine, b. March 26, 1824; William, b. Dec. 31, 1825, d. May 26, 1846; Nancy, b. March 2, 1828, m. Everett Crocker, April, 1747; Lucretia, b. June 20, 1830; Adeline, b. July 5, 1832; Charles, b. Oct. 24, 1834, d. Oct. 18, 1836; Lucy, b. March 19, 1838.

HARTHON, SOLOMON, m. JULIA A. FIELD.
Their Son,
Albert P., b. July 6, 1847.

HILL, BENJAMIN, *of New Hampshire*, m. ELIZABETH DUDLEY.
Their Children,
Nicholas D. m.   ; Sally m. 1st, Samuel Smith; 2d, Col. Samuel Sherburne, of Northwood, N. H.; Jonathan m.   ; Samuel m.   ; Noah; Judith m. Josiah Robinson.

HILL, NICHOLAS D., m.   .
Their Children,
John; Benjamin; Dudley lives at Canterbury; Mark; Walter lives at Portsmouth, N. H.; James.

HILL, JONATHAN, m.   .
Their Children,
Abraham; Jonathan; John.

HILL, SAMUEL, m.   .
Their Children,
Chase C., Esq, lives at Northwood; Edson, Esq., lives at Manchester; Dudley, and others.

HALL, JOSEPH, ESQ., m. MARY   .
Their Children,
Love, b. June 10, 1716, m. Israel Bartlet, of Newbury; Mary m. Mr. Sargeant; Sarah m. John Burleigh, of Newmarket; Rebecca m. Samuel Adams, of Durham, N. H.; Deborah m. Mr. Folsom.

HALL, EDWARD, ESQ., m. 1st, MARY WILSON.
Their Children,
Ann m. Rev. John Moody, of Newmarket, April 5, 1730, and died July 14, 1771 ; A daughter m. Rev. Mr. Page ; A daughter m. John Burgin, of Newmarket ; Jemima m. 1st, Benjamin Smith ; A daughter m. Joseph Merrill, of Stratham.

HALL, HON. KINSLEY, *of Exeter, N. H.,* m. ELIZABETH DUDLEY.
Their Children,
Josiah m. 1st, Miss Woodbury, of Beverley ; 2d,   ; Paul, b. 1689, m. Mercy   , and d. Dec. 29, 1726 ; Elizabeth m. Francis James ; Mary m. Mr. Harris, and died before her father ; Mercy m. 1st, Dudley Hilton ; 2d, Nathaniel Ladd.

HALL, JOSIAH, m. MISS WOODBURY.
Their Children,
Elizabeth m. Tobias Lear, of Portsmouth, N. H. ; Mary m. John Langdon, of P.

HALL, BENJAMIN, *of Massachusetts,* m. LUC.
Their Children,
†Lucy, d. aged about 20 years ; Dudley, Esq., l. at Medford, Mass., 1848.

HALL, JOSEPH, m. MARY HILTON.
Their Children,
Joseph, Esq., m. 1st, Mary   , who d. April 1, 1755, aged 73 years ; 2d, Eunice   , who d. March 27, 1790, aged 94 years ; Edward, Esq., m. 1st, Mary Wilson, who d. Dec. 2, 1737, aged 57 years and 22 days ; 2d, Mrs. Hannah, widow of Josiah Hall, (Miss Lord,) of Ipswich, Mass.

HILTON, COL. EDWARD, m. ANN DUDLEY.
Their Children,
Col. Winthrop, b. 1671, was killed by the Indians, June 23, 1710 ; Dudley m. Mercy Hall, dau. of Hon. Kinsley H. ; Joseph, b. at Exeter, N. H. ; Jane, b. at E. ; Judith, b. at E. ; Ann, b. at E. ; Mary m. Joseph Hall, son of Ralph H. ; Sobriety, b. at Exeter ; Bridget, b. at E.

16

HILTON, Col. Winthrop, m.
Their Daughter,
Deborah m. 1st, Samuel Thing, Dec. 26, 1722; 2d, Benjamin
Thing, Oct. 21, 1725; Bridget m. Andrew Gilman.

HILTON, Dudley, m. Mercy Hall, dau. of Hon. Kinsley H.
Their Children,
Elizabeth m. Christopher Robinson, who d. at Cape Breton; Ann
m. Nathaniel Ladd, 3d; Mary, b. at Exeter; Mercy m. Kinsley
James, Nov. 5, 1735.

HOWARD, William, *of Maine,* m. Charlotte I. Dudley.
Their Children,
George B., b. Feb. 3, 1843; Charlotte B., b. May 4, 1848.

HUBBARD, David G., m. Lucy Manwaring.
Their Children,
Hon. Wm. J. m. 1st, Eliza Chaplin, dau. of Dr. Jas. P. Chaplin, of
Cambridgeport; 2d, Deborah Payson, daughter of Hon. Moses P.
Payson, of Bath, N. Y.; David M.; Elizabeth; Martha; Charles
D.; Samuel; Harriet; Lucy m. Thomas C. Fanning, of Albion,
N. Y.; Daniel; Lydia C.

JAMES, Kinsley, *of New Hampshire,* m. Mercy Hilton.
Their Children,
Elizabeth, b. Sept. 15, 1735, d. in childhood; Mary, b. Dec. 10,
1737; Lois, b. Sept. 30, 1739, m. Theophilus Lyford; †Kinsley
H., b. 1741, d. 1810; Ann m. 1st, Thomas Lyford; 2d, Colonel
Giddings, and d. Aug. 12, 1813.

JOHNSON, Andrew, m. Asenath Dudley.
Their Children,
A son, b. at Lynn, d. in infancy; Mary S., b. at L., d. at L.

KIMBALL, John, *of New Hampshire,* m. Dorothy Dudley.
Their Children,
John; Dudley; Trueworthy m. Miss Gilman, dau. of Antipas
G., of Gilmanton; Eliphalet m. Mary Gilman, dau. of Edward G.,
Esq.; Dorothy m. John Gilman, grandson of Nehemiah Gilman;
†Betsey.

KIMBALL, Trueworthy, m. Miss Gilman.
Their Children,
John m., and probably l., in Canada West, 1848; Trueworthy m.

Miss Morrill, and l. at Nashua, N. H., 1848; Dorothy m. Samuel Eastman, of Gilmanton; Betsey m.; Joanna m. Richard Tilton, of Gilmanton.

KIMBALL, ELIPHALET, m. MARY GILMAN.
Their Children,
    Sarah, b. at Gilmanton about 1795, m. Daniel Lougee, l. at G., 1848; †Olive, b. at G. about 1798, d. about 1810 at G.; John, b. at G., 1803, m. Catharine E. Abbot, of Andover, Mass., in 1838, lives at Boston; William, b. at G., 1807, m. Augusta Stetson, of Salem; Eliphalet, b. at G. about 1817, d. in infancy; Betsey B., b. at G. about 1810, m. Lemuel Allen, of St. Johnsbury, Vt.; †Mary, b. at G. about 1818, d. about 1832, at G.

KILLAM, JOHN, *of Boxford*, m. PRISCILLA BRADSTREET.
One of their Children,
    Ann, b. March 23, 1765, m. Stephen Peabody, of Boxford, Dec. 13, 1785.

LADD, NATHANIEL, JR., m. MRS. MERCY HILTON, widow of DUDLEY H.
Their Children,
    Love; Paul; Mercy; Dudley;—all born in N. H.

LANGDON, JOHN, *of New Hampshire*, m. MARY HALL.
Their Children,
    Hon. Woodbury; Gov. John; Mary m. Mr. Storer; Elizabeth m. Mr. Barrel; Martha m. 1st, Mr. Barrel, of Simpson; 2d, Gov. James Sullivan; Abigail.

LOVELL, JOHN, *of Massachusetts*, m. ANN DUDLEY.
Their Children,
    John lived at Thompson, Conn., 1810; Mary m. Mr. Burbidge, Cornwallis, N. S.; Betsey m. Mr. Brown, of Boston.

LOVERING,* COL. THEOPHILUS, *of Raymond, N. H.*, m. SUSANNA DUDLEY.
Their Children,
    Polly, b. April 3, 1786, d. Nov. 3, 1788; John, b. March 26, 1788; Dudley, b. April 30, 1790, d. March 5, 1802; Polly, 2d, b. March 17, 1792; Abigail, b. June 16, 1796, d. Sept. 6, 1802; Gilman, b. April 5, 1795, d. July 12, 1829; Elizabeth, b. Dec. 12,

---

* Col. L. was born Jan. 3, 1759, m. Miss Dudley Jan., 1786.

1798, d. Oct. 3, 1801 ;   Dudley, 2d, b. Feb. 20, 1802, d. Feb. 12, 1808.

LOVERING, ABIJAH, m. MARY DUDLEY.
Their Children,
Lucinda ;   Warren ;   A son ;—all born at Chester, N. H.

MANWARING, DAVID, m. MARTHA SALTONSTALL.
Their Children,
William ;   Rebecca m. Elisha Coit, merchant, of N. Y. ;   Hannah ; David m. Lucy Starr ;   Martha ;   Gurdon m. Ann Adams ;   Lucy m. David G. Hubbard, merchant, of N. Y. ;   Susanna m. Gurdon Buck, merchant, of N. Y.

CHILDREN OF GURDON MANWARING.

Martha A. m. John Moore, of N. Y. ;   Mary m. Van Zandt Mumford ; Elizabeth m. J. Mason McJimsey ;   Susan m. Benjamin Babcock.

MUMFORD, DAVID, m. REBECCA SALTONSTALL.
Their Children,
David m. Ann Pearsall, of New York ;   Rebecca m. Robert Allen, of New London ;   Gurdon m. 1st, Ann Van Zandt, 2d, Letitia Van Tolen ;   †William ;   Abigail m. Thompson Phillips, of Middletown, brother of Mrs. Judge Cushing, of Scituate, Ms. ;   Thomas m. Mary Smith ;   Ann m. John Durgee, of New York ;   †John ;   Silas D. m. Ruth ———.

MILLER, JOHN, m HENRIETTA SALTONSTALL.
Their Children,
Nancy ;   Jeremiah ;   Henrietta ;   Fanny ;   Eliza ;   John m. Miss Coit ;   Gurdon m. Ann Tabor ;   Lucy m. Lieut. John Mooers.

MOODY, REV. JOHN, m. ANN HALL.
Their Daughter,
Mary, b. March 4, 1731, m. Winthrop Smith, Nov. 9, 1756.

MORRILL, CAPT. WM., m. ELIZABETH DUDLEY.
Their Children,
Frederick ;   Washington.

ORCUTT, SAMUEL, *of Maine,* m. MARTHA HARTHON.
Their Children,
Warren H., b. Sept. 7, 1839 ;   Avaluna A., b. March 27, 1842 ; Matilda, b. July 28, 1844 ;   Charles, b. March 2, 1846 ;   Eli, b. Dec. 19, 1847.   This family reside in the County of Penobscot, Me.

PAGANEL, RALPH, *of Staffordshire, Eng.*, m. ————.
Their Son,
Fulk, lord Dudley, m. Beatrix, dau. and heir of William Fitz Ausculph.

Their Son,
Ralph, lord Dudley, m. ————.

Their Son,
Gervase m. Isabel, dau. of Robert, Earl of Leicester, widow of Simon St. Liz, Earl of Northampton, l. 1133, at Dudley Castle.

Their Children,
Robert, who, it is presumed, d. young; Hawyse m. 1st, John de Somerie, 2d, Roger de Berkley, of Berkley Castle.

PAGE, WILLIAM H., m. MARY A. DUDLEY.
Their Children,
Caroline; Albert; Dudley; Anna.

PARKER, MAJ. NATHANIEL, *of Massachusetts*, m. REBECCA DUDLEY.
Their Children,
Nathaniel, Jr., b. March 3, 1789; Thomas, b. May 27, 1791; Penuel, b. Aug. 17, 1793; Warren, b. 1795, m. Nancy Wales; William, b. Jan. 28, 1798, m. Anna Leeds; George W.; Hannah, b. Feb. 2, 1804, m. Ebenezer Holden, Oct. 16, 1823, and lives at Dorchester, Ms.

PEABODY,* JOSEPH, *of Topsfield*, m. ELIZABETH BRADSTREET.
Their Children,
Joseph, b. Sept. 15, 1730, d. Aug. 7, 1736; Jacob, b. Dec. 2, 1731, d. Aug. 14, 1736; Dudley, b. June 15, 1735, d. Aug. 6, 1736; Elizabeth, b. Sept. 23, 1737, d. Dec. 20, 1806; Jacob, 2d, b. April 6, 1739, m. Sarah Potter, 1763, d. Nov. 25, 1806; Priscilla, b. 1743, m. Isaac Averill, Dec. 22, 1761; Margaret, b. April 13, 1748, m. Benjamin Bixby, Jr., Oct. 9, 1770.

PEABODY, SAMUEL, m. MARY BRADSTREET.
Their Children,
Samuel P., b. Nov. 27, 1820; Stephen, b. Jan. 25, 1822; Mary A., b. Sept. 1, 1823; Melissa, b. Nov. 2, 1824; Caroline E., b. April 21, 1826; Albert B., b. Nov. 1, 1828.

---

* Mr. Peabody was born June 14, 1704, and died June 7, 1755.

PEABODY, Stephen, *of Boxford*, m. Ann Killam.
Their Children,
Stephen ;   Samuel, b. Nov. 6, 1788 ;   Nancy, b. Aug. 28, 1796.

PHILBRICK, Rev. Peter, *of Deerfield*, *N. H.*, m. Betsey Dudley.
Their Children,
Elizabeth A. G., b. March 9, 1816 ;   Peter H., b. March 26, 1817, d. Feb. 20, 1835, at Raymond ;   John D., b. May 27, 1819, grad. at Dart. Coll., m. Julia A. Putman, of Danvers, Mass., lives at Boston ;   A son, b. 1823, d. 1824 ;—they were all born at Deerfield.

PERKINS, Nehemiah, *of Topsfield*, m. Lydia Bradstreet.
Their Children,
Lydia, b. April 5, 1818 ;   Nehemiah, b. Nov. 8, 1820 ;   Phebe W., b. Oct. 21, 1822 ;   Benjamin A., b. June 12, 1824 ;   Moses, b. June 17, 1826 ;   Ruth L., b. Jan. 1, 1828 ;   Esther G., b. July 29, 1831 ;   Albert C., b. Dec. 18, 1833 ;   Eliza B., b. June 8, 1835 ;   John W., b. Aug. 21, 1841.

PERRYMAN, Nicholas, Esq.,* *of Exeter*, *N. H.*, m. Joanna Dudley.
Their Children,
John, b. Aug. 30, 1718, d. 1736 ;   Joanna, b. Nov. 14, 1731, m. Noah Emery, Esq., who was b. Dec. 23, 1731, and she d. April, 1814 ;   Sarah, b. July 9, 1720, d. June, 1721 ;   Nicholas, b. July, 1734, d. Aug. 22, 1736.

PILLSBURY,§ Ebenezer, Esq., m. Eliza Dudley, Sept. 14, 1815.
Their Children,
Susan J., b. June 13, 1816, d. Jan. 30, 1817 ;   Caleb D., b. Dec. 13, 1818, m. Orphia M. Curtis, Nov. 7, 1840 ;   Wm. King, b. Jan. 21, 1820, d. March 7, 1836 ;   Daniel W., b. Aug. 24, 1822, m. Selina E. Porter, Nov. 17, 1844 ;   Eben F., b. April 18, 1825, m. Ruth S. Dolbier, Dec. 3, 1846 ;   Charles F., b. Jan. 31, 1828 ;   Lucien B., b. April 21, 1830 ;   Eliza E., b. March 4, 1833.   They were born at Kingfield, Me.

PUTMAN, Ahira H., *of Mass.*, m. Sarah Bradstreet.
Their Children,
Granville B., b. Aug. 31, 1835 ;   Wallace d. young ;   Wallace A., b. Feb. 23, 1838.

---

* He was born Dec. 24, 1692, and died Aug. 9, 1757.
§ Mr. Pillsbury was b. June 7, 1790, and Mrs. Pillsbury was b. Dec. 20, 1791.

RICHARDS, Dr. Joseph, *of Mass.*, m. Elizabeth Dudley.*

Their Children,

Paul D., merchant, b. Jan. 7, 1750, at Dedham, Mass., m. Anna Mayo,§ of Roxbury, June 20, 1776, and d. Jan. 6, 1822, at Boston ; William, farmer, b. June 26, 1753, m. Sally Tileston. of Dorchester, and d. at Dorchester ; ‡Joel, b. Dec. 18, 1758, m. Prudence Swett, 1784, and died Oct. 4, 1837, at Claremont, N. H., aged 79 years. The wife died about 1833.

RICHARDS, Paul D., m. Anna Mayo.

Their Children,

Joseph, merchant, b. Nov. 27, 1777, at Boston, m. Alice W. Lovering, of Boston, Oct. 4, 1800, and d. April 15, 1822, at Boston ; Elizabeth, b. Aug. 18, 1781, at B., m. Richards Child, merchant, (who d. Nov. 28, 1840, at B.,) and l. at Boston, 1848.

RICHARDS, Joseph, m. Alice W. Lovering.

Their Children,

Esther, b. Aug. 17, 1801, at Boston, m. C. W. Apthorp, merchant, of B. ; Elizabeth, b. March 9, 1803, at Boston, d. Sept. 28, 1805 ; Anna M., b. Jan. 28, 1805, at B., d. Oct. 10, 1805 ; Elizabeth A., b. July 7, 1806, m. 1st, Charles S. Tewksbury, merchant of Troy, N. Y. ; 2d, Benj. H. Reed, merchant of Worcester, Mass. ; Paul D., b. Dec. 19, 1808, at B., m. Elizabeth Whipple, Dec. 29, 1835 ; Nancy L., b. Sept. 28, 1810, d. Dec. 5, 1811, at B. ; Joseph L., b. June 3, 1812, at B., m. Mary G. Ballard, Oct. 29, 1835 ; Joel, b. July 29, 1814, at B., merchant, m. Caroline R. Lakeman, July 20, 1836 ; Nancy C., b. Jan. 10, 1817, at B., m. Theodore H. Dorr, of Billerica, and afterwards of Lexington, Mass. ; William, b. June 14, 1819, at B., m. Julia Pray, of Climax, Mich. ; George K., b. March 27, 1822, at B., m. Nancy Mallard, of Lancaster, Mass.

ROGERS, Dr. John, *of Ipswich,* m. Elizabeth Dennison.

Their Children,

Elizabeth, b. Feb. 26, 1661 ; Margaret, b. Feb. 18, 1664 ; Rev. John, b. July 7, 1666, at Ipswich, grad. at H. C., 1684, m. Martha Whittingham, dau. of John W., March 4, 1691, and d. Dec. 28, 1745 ; Dr. Daniel, b. Sept. 25, ——, at I., grad. at H. C., 1686, d. in a severe snow-storm, on Hampton Beach, Dec. 1, 1722 ; Rev.

---

* This lady m , secondly, Samuel Scarboro', but they had no issue.

§ Miss Anna was born Sept. 20, 1756, and died Oct. 9, 1825, at Boston.

Nathaniel, b. Feb. 22, 1670, lived at Portsmouth, N. H., grad. at H. C., 1687, d. Oct. 3, 1723 ; Patience, b. May 25, 1676.

THE CHILDREN OF Rev. JOHN ROGERS.

Rev. John, b. Jan. 19, 1692, grad. at H.C., 1711, settled at Eliot, Me., d. Oct. 16, 1773 ; Martha ; Rev. Nathaniel, b. March 4, 1702, grad. at H. C., 1721, lived at Ipswich, d. in 1775 ; Richard, b. Dec. 2, 1703, was a merchant of Ipswich ; Elizabeth ; Rev. Daniel, b. July 28, 1707, grad. at H. C., in 1725, lived at Exeter, N. H., d. Dec. 9, 1785, Elizabeth, 2d,—twins ; Dr. Samuel, b. Aug. 31, 1709, grad. at H. C., 1725, d. at Ipswich, Dec. 21, 1772.

THE CHILDREN OF Dr. DANIEL ROGERS.

Rev. Daniel, of Littleton, grad. at H. C., 1725, d. Nov. 1782, aged 76. *Others*, whose names are unknown.

THE CHILDREN OF Dea. NATHANIEL ROGERS.

Dr. Nathaniel, grad. at H. C., 1717, d. Nov. 15, 1746 ; Hon. Daniel, member of the Royal Council of N. H. *Others*, doubtless, names unknown.

RUMRILL, Thomas, *of Roxbury, Mass.,* m. Mrs. Sally Fellows, *widow of John W. Fellows.*
Their Children,

Sarah D. m. Henry Robinson, lived at Roxbury, 1848 ; Elizabeth C. m. George Young, lived at R., 1848 ; John W. F., d. in childhood, at R. ; †Thomas, Jr. ; William m. Nancy Young, lived at R., 1848 ; Lucretia, d. in childhood.

SALTONSTALL, Gurdon, *Son of Gov. S., of Conn.,* m. Rebecca Winthrop.
Their Children,

Gurdon, died unmarried ; Rebecca m. David Mumford, merchant, of New London ; Catharine m. John Richards, merchant, of do. ; Winthrop m. Ann Wanton, dau. of Gov. Wanton ; Dudley m. Francis Babcock ; Ann m. Thomas Mumford, of Norwich ; Rosewell m. Elizabeth Stewart ; Elizabeth m. 1st, Mr. Ebbets, of New York, 2d, Silas Deane, of Wethersfield, Minister to France ; Mary m. Jeremiah Atwater, of New Haven ; Richard died unmarried ; Martha m. David Manwaring, of New London ; Henrietta m. John Miller ; Gilbert m. Harriet Babcock ; Sarah m. Daniel Buck, of Wethersfield, Ct.

SALTONSTALL, CHILDREN OF WINTHROP.

Rebecca m. Peter Christophers, of New London; Gurdon m. Hannah Sage; Mary m. Dr. Thomas Coit, of New London; †Winthrop; †Ann.

SALTONSTALL, CHILDREN OF DUDLEY.

Hannah m. Mr. Walley; †Fanny; Dudley m. Miss Chapin; †Thomas; Catharine m. Dr. Dugan, of Canandagua, N. Y.; Joshua m. Miss Lewis; Martha m. Mr. Stoddard.

SALTONSTALL, CHILDREN OF ROSEWELL.

Abigail m. Dr. Handy, of New York; Mary m. Mr. Fell; †Elizabeth; †Richard; †Hannah; †Francis; Rosewell m.   ; Francis m.   .

SALTONSTALL, CHILDREN OF GILBERT.

Gilbert m. Miss Starr; Gurdon.

SEAVER, John, *of Roxbury*, m. Betsey Dudley.
Their Children,

John C. m. Mary Shepard, lives at Roxbury; Elizabeth D. m. Jeremiah Locke, lives at Stetson, Me.; William D. m. Catharine Hobbs, lives at Roxbury; Harriet, d. in infancy; Henry m., and lives in Canada East; Harriet, d. in childhood; Maria m. Joseph Houghton, lives at R.; †Adeline, lives at R.; Sarah A. m. Jeremiah B. Clement, lives at Boston; †Caroline, lives at Roxbury.

SEWALL, Samuel, Jr., Esq., m. Rebecca Dudley.
Their Children,

Rebecca, b. 1704, d. Aug. 3, 1710; Samuel, b. Nov. 18, 1707, d. Dec. 18, 1708; Hannah, b. Oct. 25, 1709, d. Oct. 21, 1719; Mary, b. July 20, 1711, d. Aug. 25, 1712; Henry, b. March 8, 1720, grad. at H. C., in 1738, m. Ann White, of Brookline, Aug. 18, 1743, and d. May 29, 1771, at Brookline; John, b. April 9, 1723, probably died young. They were all born at Brookline, Mass.

The Children of Henry and Ann Sewall.

Hull, b. April 9, 1744, grad. at H. C., 1761, m. Abigail Sparhawk, of Little Cambridge, now Brighton, and d. Nov. 27, 1767; †Samuel, Esq., b. Dec. 31, 1745, grad. at H. C., 1761, was a royalist, and went to England, 1776, where he d. at the city of Bristol, May 6, 1811; †Henry, Jr., b. Jan. 19, 1749, grad. at H. C., in 1768, d.

17

Oct. 17, 1772; Hannah, b. Sept. 2, 1751, m. Edward Wolcott, of Brookline, and d. a widow at the house of her daughter, Mrs. Phillip R. Ridgeway, in Dorchester, 1832, aged 81 years.

SIDNEY, Sir Henry,[*] K. G., *Lord Deputy of Ireland and President of Wales,* m. Mary Dudley.
Their Children,
Sir Phillip, Kt., b. Nov. 24, 1554, was slain in the battle of Zutphen, Oct. 16, 1586; his wife was Frances Walsingham, dau. and heir of Sir Francis W. This lady m. 2dly, Robert Devereux, Earl of Essex, 3dly, Richard, Earl of Clanricard; Sir Robert, Kt., Lord Sidney, of Penhurst, Viscount L'Isle, and first Earl of Leicester, m. 1st, Barbara Gamage, dau. and heir of Sir Thomas G. of Coyly, in Glamorganshire; 2dly, the widow of Sir Thomas Smith, Kt., and d. July 13, 1626, at Penhurst; Thomas m. Margaret Dakins, dau. and heir of Arthur D., who m. 2dly, Sir Thomas Hobby, Kt.; Mary m. Henry, Earl of Pembroke.

SIDNEY, Sir Phillip, m. Francis Walsingham.
Their Daughter,
Elizabeth m. Roger Manners, Earl of Rutland.

SIDNEY, Sir Robert, m. Barbara Gamage.
Their Children,
‡Sir William, K. B.; Henry, and Phillip, d. in infancy; Sir Robert, K. P., second Earl of Leicester, m. Dorothy Percy, dau. of Henry P., Earl of Northumberland, and d. 1677; Mary m. Sir Robert Wroth, Kt.; Catharine m. Sir Lucas Mansell, Kt.; Phillis m. Sir John Hubbard, Kt.; Barbara; Elizabeth; Bridget; Alice; and Vere.

SLACK, Lewis, *of Roxbury,* m. Pedy Dudley.
Their Children,
William D., b. Feb. 18, 1834, at Roxbury; George A., b. April 24, 1838, at R.

SMITH, Winthrop, *of N. H.,* m. Mary Moody.
Their Children,
John M., Esq.; Ezra; Eliphalet; Joseph; Nancy; Polly and Andrew.

---

[*] Sir Henry d. March 5, 1586, and was buried at Penhurst. His wife, Mary, d. Aug. 9, 1586.

SOMERIE, John de, m. Hawise Paganel.
Their Son,
Ralph, feudal lord of Dudley, m.   , d. 1210.
Their Children,
William Perceval, Baron of Dudley, m.   , d. 1221 ; Roger,
l. in the reign of Henry III, m. and d. 1271.

THE SON OF WILLIAM PERCEVAL, Baron of Dudley.
‡Nicholas, Baron of Dudley, d. 1228.

HIS UNCLE, ROGER, Baron of Dudley, m. 1st, Nicola,
dau. of William de Albine, the second Earl of Arundel. This
lady was a sister and co-heir of Hugh, fourth Earl of Arundel.
2d, Amabel, dau. and heir of Sir Robert de Chaucombe, Kt., and
widow of Gilbert de Legrave.

SOMERIE, CHILDREN OF ROGER De, last named.
By his first wife,
Joane m. John le Strange ; Mabel m. Walter de Sulcy ; Maud
m. Henry de Erdington ; Margery m. 1st, Ralph Cromwell, of
Tatshal, 2d, William Bifield.
By his second wife,
Roger m.   , d. 1290 ; John ; Margaret m. Ralph Basset,
of Drayton.

SOMERIE, CHILDREN OF ROGER De, Son of Roger de
Somerie.
Roger, feudal lord of Dudley, d. in youth ; ‡Sir John, K. B.,
member of Parliament from March 10, 1308, to March 14, 1322,
as Baron, d. 1322 ; Margaret m. John de Sutton, first Baron of
Dudley, of that name ; Joan, co-heiress, with her sister Margaret
of the castle of Dudley.

THING, Benjamin, *of N. H.,* m. Deborah Hilton.
Their Children,
Pernal, b. July 29, 1726, m. Rev. Nath'l Trask ; Winthrop, b.
Jan. 10, 1728 ; Mary, b. May 24, 1730, m. Z. Clough, Esq., of
Poplin ; Ann, b. Oct. 18, 1732, m. Col. Samuel Folsom, of E. ;
Samuel, b. Dec. 13, 1735 ; Elizabeth, b. Sept. 2, 1740. They
were all born at Exeter, N. H.

THING, John, *of Brentwood, N. H.,* m. Ann Dudley.
Their Children,
Levi, b. at Brentwood, N. H., 1661, m. Susan Sanborn, dau. of
Abram S. ; Samuel, b. at B., 1663, m. Hannah Smith ; John, b.
at B., 1665, m. Mercy Rundlett ; Nancy, b. at B., 1667, m. Jonathan

Norris; Dudley L , b. at B , May 23, 1770, m. Rachel Sanborn, dau. of Abram S., 1790; Abigail, b. at B., 1772, m. Samuel Calley; Mary, b. at B., 1774, m. Mr. Bartlett.

THING, DUDLEY L., *of Industry, Me.*, m. RACHEL SANBORN.
Their Children,
Capt. Joseph, b. Jan. 25, 1791, at Brentwood, m. 1st, Abigail Brown, 1818, 2d, Mary Allen, March 20, 1830, lives at Boston, Ms. ; Jonathan, b. Aug. 15, 1792, at B. ; Samuel, b. May 13, 1795, at B. ; Nancy, b. Aug. 8, 1799, at B. ; John, b. April 9, 1802, at B. ; David, b. Aug. 18, 1804, at B.; Rev. Dudley, b. March 7, 1806, at B. ; Jesse, b. Aug. 22, 1808, at B., m. Mary R. Allen, who died Dec. 18, 1847, lives at Industry, Me. ; Elizabeth, b. March 31, 1813, at B.

THING, JESSE, m. MARY R. ALLEN.
Their Children,
Christiana A., b. May 15, 1831; Elvira D., b. Feb. 26, 1834 ; David O., b. Nov. 6, 1838 ; Mary A., b. Aug. 12, 1841 ; Billings A., b. Oct. 31, 1844 ; Datus A., b. Feb. 14, 1847.

THURSTON, CALEB, m. HANNAH DUDLEY.
Their Children,
Caleb ; John, of Maine ; Dudley, of Monmouth, Me. ; Daniel ; Trueworthy, of Maine ; Sarah ; Hannah m. Samuel Hopkinson.

TUCKER, BARNARD, *of Raymond, N. H.,* m. SALLY DUDLEY.
Their Children,
· Philena A. m. Edward Sumner, of Roxbury, Ms. ; Moses D. ; James M. ; John D. ; Isaac ; Nancy ; Sarah ; Jane ; Hellen.

TUCKER, GEN. HENRY, *of Raymond,* m. NANCY DUDLEY.
Their Children,
Josephine L., b. Feb. 28, 1828, lives at Boston ; Gilman H., b. Jan. 20. 1836 ; Abby A. D., b. Aug. 14, 1843.

TREAT, JOHN, *of Maine,* m. MRS. LUCY WINSLOW, dau. of Capt. Samuel Bailey, and they had a daughter Mary E.

TUFTS, DR. SIMON, m. LUCY DUDLEY.
Their Children,
Simon, b. at Medford, Mass., d. about 1802, at the Cape of Good Hope ; Lucy, b. at M., m. Benjamin Hall, merchant, of Medford.

WANTON, Gov. Joseph, m. *A Daughter of* Hon. Wait Still Winthrop.
Their Children,
Joseph ; William ; a daughter m. Thomas Wickham, of Newport ; one m. Gov. Brown, of Bermuda, a cousin ; one m. Dr. Destalieur, surgeon in the English Army ; one m. Winthrop Saltonstall, of New London, Ct. ; one m. Mr. Codington, of Newport.

WEBSTER, Col. Ebenezer, *of Maine,* m. Lucy Dudley.
Their Children,
Martha, b. Aug. 17, 1806, at Oldtown, Me., m. Joseph Treat ; Alexander, b. June 5, 1808, d. Oct. 22, 1809 ; Lucy, b. Aug. 7, 1810, m. Josiah Bennoch ; Ebenezer, b. May 21, 1812, m. Martha A. Trafton ; Paul D., b. Sept. 3, 1814, m. Lucina M. Crowell, Sept. 22, 1842, at Dexter, Me. She was born July 20, 1825 ; Ann B., b. July 17, 1816, m. Dr. William H. Allen ; Susan H., b. Jan. 1, 1819, m. William Avery, Oct. 24, 1841 ; Catharine B., b. March 7, 1821, m. Nathan Weston, Esq., of Orono, Me. ; Mary M., b. July 24, 1824, m. Israel Washburn, Esq., Oct. 24, 1841.

WEBSTER, Paul D., m. Lucina M. Crowell.
Their Children,
Mary L., b. July 4, 1843 ; Ebenezer P., b. Dec. 23, 1845 ; Charles M., b. Dec. 5, 1847.

WESTON, Nathan, Esq., *of Penobscot Co. Me.,* m. Catharine B. Webster.
Their Children,
Martha P. ; Nathan ; Charles M.

WASHBURN, Israel, Esq., m. Mary M. Webster.
Their Children,
Israel H. ; and Ada.—born at Orono, Me.

WHITING, Seth T., m. Lucy Dudley.
Their Children,
Lucy, b. at Roxbury, m. Joseph Hay, of Boston, whose first wife was her sister Bathsheba, l. at B., 1848 ; Ebenezer, b. and d. at Roxbury ; Bathsheba, b. at R., m. Joseph Hay ; †Seth T., Jr., b. and d. at R. ; †George, b. and d. at R.

WILLIAMS, Henry H., m. Mary Dudley.
Their Children,
Henry H., Jr. ; Thomas D., Elbridge G. D. This family were

born at Roxbury, and are now living there. The dates of their births I have been unable to obtain.

WINSLOW, NATHAN, *of Maine*, m. LUCY BAILEY.
Their Children,
Charles ; Nathan, Jr.

WINTHROP, JOHN, F. R. S., *Son of Hon. Wait Still, grandson of Gov. John, of Conn., and great-grandson of Gov. John, of Massachusetts Bay*, m. ANN DUDLEY.
Their Children,
John Still, b. Jan. 15, 1720, at New London, Ct., m. 1st, Jane Borland, of Boston, dau. of Francis B., Sept. 4, 1750, 2d, a dau. of William Sheriff, and d. at N. L., June 6, 1776 ; Basil ; A daughter m. Gov. Wanton, of R. I. ; One m. 1st, Mr. Brown, of Salem, 2d, Mr. Sargent, of Salem ; One m. Mr. Jeremiah Miller, of New London ; Rebecca, m. Gurdon Saltonstall, son of Gov. S. of Connecticut ; Ann d. unmarried.

WINTHROP, THE CHILDREN OF JOHN STILL.
By first wife,
John, grad. at H. C., 1770 ; Jane ; Francis B., d. at New York, leaving four sons and three daughters ; Ann m. David Sears, Esq., of Boston ; William, Esq., of New York ; Joseph, of Charleston, S. C., d. 1828 ; Mary ; Lieut. Gov. Thomas L., b. at New London, March, 1760.
By the second wife,
Benjamin, of New York, m. a dau. of Peter Stuyvessant, Esq. ; Robert, an Admiral in the British Navy ; Elizabeth Sebor, of Middletown, Connecticut.

WINTHROP, HON. THOMAS L., LL. D., m. ELIZABETH BOWDOIN, *dau. of Sir John Temple, baronet, and grand-daughter of Gov. Bowdoin.*
Their Children,
Elizabeth B. T. ; Sarah B. ; Thomas L. ; Augusta T. ; Augusta T., 2d ; James Bowdoin ; John T. ; Francis Wm. ; Francis Wm., 2d ; Jane ; Ann ; George Edward ; Grenville T. ; Robert C., Speaker of the House of Representatives in Congress.

WOODBRIDGE, REV. JOHN, *Son of Rev. John W., was born at Stanton, in Wiltshire, Eng.*, 1613. He first came to this country with his uncle, Rev. Thomas Parker, in 1634. His wife was MERCY DUDLEY, dau. of Gov. Thomas Dudley.

Their Children,

Sarah, b. 1640; Lucy, b. 1642; Rev. John, Jr., grad. at H. C., 1664, settled at Killingworth, Conn., in 1666, removed to Wethersfield, in 1679, where he d. 1690; Rev. Benjamin, b. at Bristol, R. I., ; .   ., m. Mary Ward, dau. of Rev. John W., of Haverhill, and l. at Kittery, Me., in 1688, d. at Medford, Jan. 15, 1710; Rev. Timothy, b. in England, grad. at H. C., 1675, settled at Hartford Centre, Conn., in 1685, and d. April 30, 1732, aged nearly 80 years; Capt. Thomas, b. 1649, m. Mary Jones, 1672, and d. at Newbury, Ms., March 2, 1681; Joseph m. Martha Rogers, grand-daughter of Rev. Nathaniel R., May 20, 1686; Martha m. Capt. Samuel Ruggles, of Roxbury. There were four others, names unknown.

WOODBRIDGE, THE SON OF REV. JOHN, Jr., *of Wethersfield.*

Rev. John, 3d, b. 1678, grad. at H. C., 1694, m. Jemima Eliot, dau. of Rev. Joseph E., of Guilford, Ct., and d. June 10, 1718, at West Springfield.

The Son of Rev. John Woodbridge, 3d,

Rev. Ephraim, grad. at H. C., 1701, m. Miss H. Morgan, 1704, and the same year settled at Jewett's City, Ct.; d. 1724.

The eldest son of the last, viz :

Dudley, m. Sarah Sheldon, 1729, and they had Dudley, who m. Miss Backus, of Norwich, Ct., and Elizabeth, who m. Daniel Rodman, of New York.

Daniel and Elizabeth Rodman's

Elizabeth W., m, *Andrew Backus, of New York, and they had* Frederick R., iron merchant, of Philadelphia, who m. Susanna Keyser, dau. of Rev. Peter K., of Philadelphia; †Philip M., of Boom Eliza G., who m. William Stuart, Esq., of New York; Isabella S., who m. William Adams, of Chicago, Ill.

William W. m. Lucy Woodbridge, and they are living at Stonington, Ct.

Thomas W. m. Ann Robinson, and both are deceased, leaving a daughter, Lucy Ann; Daniel m. Eliza Jenkins, both deceased, leaving Adelaide, who m. Mr. Newkirk, of Oswego, N. Y., and Laura, who m. William Pardee, of Oswego; Lucy W. m. Rev. Phillip F. Mayer, D.D., of Philadelphia, and both are living; Julia m. Rev. John Goodman, of Philadelphia, and is deceased, leaving Catharine, Charlotte, and Julia.

WOODBRIDGE, Joseph, m. Martha Rogers.
Their Children,
Joseph, Jr., b. 1687; Nathaniel, b. 1696; others, names unknown.

CHILDREN OF FREDERICK R. BACKUS.
William R., b. Jan. 15, 1828; Kate Clemens, b. Sept. 21, 1831; Frederick B., b. Dec. 27, 1833; Mary E., b. March 8, 1838.

WOODWARD, Capt. Alexander, m. Lucretia Bailey.
Their Children,
Albert A.; Martha F.; Nancy B.; Oscar; Lucy W.;—all born in Penobscot Co., Me.

YOUNG, Aaron, m. Abigail Dudley.
Their Children,
Dudley, b. Feb. 20, 1739, m. Margaret Smith, and d. Nov. 22, 1802; Aaron, Jr., b. Aug. 3, 1746, m. Dorothy Young, dau. of Hezekiah Y., and d. 1814, at Union, Me.; Abigail, b. Oct 2, 1748, m. John Hook; Sarah, b. Feb. 28, 1751, m. Samuel Dudley, Jr.; David, b. May, 1753, m. Elizabeth Clark, 1779, and d. 1826; Jonathan, b. Jan. 12, 1756, m. Sarah Clifford.

YOUNG, Aaron, Jr., m. Dorothy Young.
Their Children,
Joanna, b. Dec. 19, 1769, m. Mr. Bartlet; Joseph, b. Oct. 10, 1772, m. Miss Bartlet; John,* b. Dec. 23, 1775, m. Polly Mace; Aaron, 3d, b. Dec. 17, 1778, m. Miss Prue; Jonathan, b. March 6, 1781, m. Miss Towle; Mary, b. May 17, 1783; Dorothy, b. Nov. 12, 1785; Betsey, b. May 18, 1788; David, b. Oct. 3, 1790; Peter, b. July 25, 1793; Hannah, b. July 11, 1795; Sally, b. Dec. 29, 1797.

---

* John Young, son of Aaron, Jr., had a very numerous family.

INDEX.

HEADS OF FAMILIES BY THE NAMES OF

SUTTON AND DUDLEY.

18

INDEX OF NAMES.

144

INDEX OF NAMES.

Thing, Jesse, 136
Thing, John, 29, 136
Thing, Jonathan, 29
Thing, Josiah, 24
Thing, Mr., 23
Thing, Samuel, 125
Threlkeld, Lancelot, Esq., 9
Thurston, Caleb, 27, 136,
Tilton, John, 58
Tilton, Joseph, Esq., 123
Tilton, Richard, 127
Tilton, Samuel, 53
Torrey, Daniel, 102
Totman, John, 101
Treat, John, 136
Treat, Joseph, 137
Tucker, Barnard, 52, 136
Tucker, Gen. Henry, 52, 136
Tufts, Dr. Simon, 84, 136
Tufts, Capt. Peter, 121
Viles, John, 95
Wade, Maj. Nathl., 117

Wainwright, Francis, 84
Walker, Asa, 106
Walker, Jonathan, 93
Wanton, Gov. Joseph, 137
Ward, Arthur, 59
Ward, Humble, 14
Warner, Caleb, 123
Washburn, Eli, 96
Washburn, Israel, Esq., 137
Waters, Salmon, 106
Watson, Mr., 21, 23
Webb, Samuel, 61
Webster, Col. Ebenezer, 86, 137
Webster, Paul D., 137
Webster, Waldron, 32
Wells, Nathaniel, 36
Weston, Nathan, Esq., 137
Wheeler, Joel, 101
Whipple, Ebenezer, 106
White, Stephen, 119
Whiting, Rev. John, 121
Whiting, Seth T., 85, 137

Whitney,
Wickham, Thomas, 137
Wiggin, Hon. Andrew, 117
Wiggin, Mr., of Exeter, 117
Wildes, Elisha, 118
Willey, Wm. T., 194
Williams, Henry H., 88, 137
Williams, Rev. Wm., 121
Wilmer, Thomas, Esq., 13
Winslow, Nathan, 138
Winthrop, Hon. Thomas L., 138
Winthrop, John, Esq., 84, 138
Winthrop, John Still, Esq., 139
Wolcott, Edward, 134
Woodbridge, Joseph, 140
Woodbridge, Rev. John, 19, 138, 139
Woodward, Capt. Alex., 140
Wroth, Sir Robert, 134
Young, Aaron, 26, 140
Young, George, 132